A JOURNEY IN WINE

CORNWALL TO McLAREN VALE

A JOURNEY IN WINE

CORNWALL TO McLAREN VALE

Angove Family Winemakers since 1886

Geoffrey C. Bishop

Wakefield Press

Angove Family Winemakers
PO Box 12
Renmark
South Australia 5341
www.angove.com.au

in association with

Wakefield Press
1 The Parade West
Kent Town
South Australia 5067
www.wakefieldpress.com.au

First published 2012

Proudly designed and published in South Australia

Designed by Lahn Stafford Design, Adelaide
Printed and bound by Hyde Park Press, Adelaide

National Library of Australia Cataloguing-in-Publication entry

Bishop, Geoffrey C.
A journey in wine: Cornwall to McLaren Vale: Angove Family Winemakers
since 1886 / Geoffrey C. Bishop.

ISBN 978 1 74305 023 1 (pbk.).

Angove family.
Wine and wine making – South Australia – McLaren Vale – History.
McLaren Vale Region (S. Aust.) – History.
South Australia – Genealogy.
Cornwall (England: County) – Genealogy.

929.2099423

Contents

Foreword

The year 2011 marks two significant milestones for Angove Family Winemakers. The first is our 125th anniversary. In 1886, the Angove family wine journey began when my great-grandfather, Dr William Thomas Angove, and his family settled at Tea Tree Gully, then a small rural township in the foothills north of Adelaide. Dr Angove established a small vineyard and winery on his property and began making wine. Initially they were as a 'tonic' for his patients but within 10 years his hobby had grown to such an extent it became the family business.

The second milestone is the celebration of 100 years of winemaking and distilling at our Renmark winery. In 1911, the second generation of the family, my grandfather, Thomas 'Skipper' Angove, commenced the first ever winery on the River Murray at Renmark in South Australia. The original wooden vats and distillery have changed greatly since his day and the site is now occupied by a state-of-the-art winery producing fine wines and brandies.

Through world wars, economic depressions, floods, fires, industry corporatisation and consolidation, vine pull schemes and compulsory acquisition of our vineyards we have survived and thrived and remain proudly independent, family owned and operated. We could not have achieved all of this without the ongoing support and commitment of our family and friends, including all who work, and have worked, with us over the past 125 years and all of our long-standing customers and consumers both in Australia and around the world.

The challenges facing the Australian wine industry continue and we have not been immune to these, but in celebrating our 125th year, we are focused on our future.

Across our range of fine wines and brandies we continue to win accolades from the industry and consumers. We are very proud to be marking our anniversary by releasing the first vintage of Angove Family Winemakers' The Medhyk, an ultra premium Shiraz that pays homage to our founder. This exemplary, limited release wine has been sourced from old Shiraz vines in McLaren Vale from the vintage of 2008. We are new arrivals in this region but have been sourcing grapes from McLaren Vale for a number of years for one of our Vineyard Select wines. We have recently purchased a significant vineyard in the region and will be developing an exciting new cellar door during 2011. The vineyard will provide premium fruit for limited release wines.

We continue to develop our comprehensive portfolio of wine and spirit offerings and our productive working relationships with our agency companies and distributors around the world.

Our aim is to further develop our exceptional quality wines from the finest vineyards. That's the bond we all share, a driving passion to craft outstanding, enjoyable wines from premium regions and grape varieties.

We are proud of our past and look forward to building on our company's tradition and progressiveness into the future.

John Angove *Chairman and Managing Director, Angove Family Winemakers*

Preface

In 1886 Cornish-born Dr William Thomas Angove left England to settle with his wife and young family at Tea Tree Gully, South Australia. His father, Thomas Angove, was a mining man, as had been many earlier generations of the family, but William chose not to follow in his father's profession. He studied medicine in London, and after a decade in private practice at Mildenhall, Suffolk, decided to seek a medical practice in South Australia. Once settled at the township of Tea Tree Gully near Adelaide, his interests apart from medicine gained full expression. Not least amongst these was an interest in grape growing and winemaking.

Dr Angove continued to practise medicine at Tea Tree Gully until his death (in England) in 1912 by which time his winemaking activities had expanded to become a family business as Angove & Sons, St Agnes Vineyards. The family went on to pioneer winemaking in the Riverland of South Australia, and despite the disruptions of River Murray floods, two world wars, an economic depression and significant changes to wine exporting, Angove developed a fine reputation for premium quality wine and brandy.

This is the remarkable story of that business, currently carried on by the fourth and fifth generation members of the Angove family as Angove Family Winemakers.

The story of the first 100 years of Angove Family Winemakers is largely based on documents and other written records with some material derived from interviews with company employees and family members. To a large extent, this history does not overly repeat material that appeared in the company's centenary publication, *Mining, Medicine and Winemaking – A History of the Angove Family 1886–1986*. In contrast to the first 100 years, the events of the past 25 years are largely told through the words of members of the Angove family and Angove Family Winemakers' employees. It has been a period of reassessment of their operations, followed by the repositioning of the company in the wine industry. As a privately-owned company, Angove Family Winemakers has been able to take a long-term view of where it wanted to be by its 125th anniversary and beyond. There is an immense pride within the Angove family and their employees in the company and the high quality of the wine and brandy they produce.

The company strives, at all times, to represent its vision to be a world-class winemaker and marketer of global brands. These guiding principles have shaped the company as an employer, and in its involvement with other sectors of the wine industry and with the local community. Whilst researching this history, some comments came up time and time again, regarding how the company's employees feel about working for the family business. The remarks were summed up well by one employee, 'There's a whole cultural shift that John [Angove] has brought to the company. It's really a family winery; John is responsible for our families as well as his own, in the broadest sense. Our people refer to our vineyards, our winery, our wines – the staff have a true sense of ownership.'

Geoffrey C. Bishop *April 2011*

Abridged Angove
Family Tree

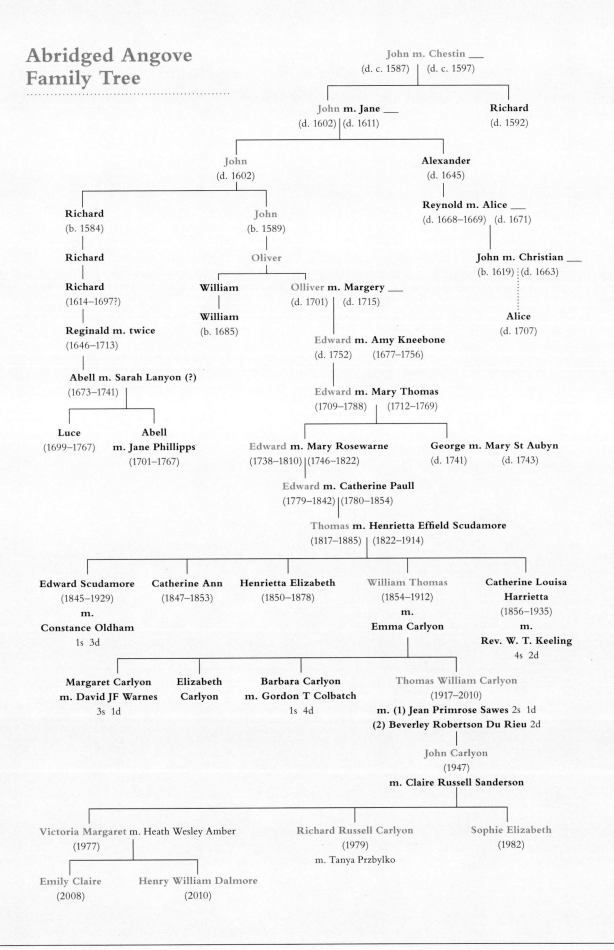

John m. Chestin ___
(d. c. 1587) | (d. c. 1597)

John m. Jane ___
(d. 1602) | (d. 1611)

Richard
(d. 1592)

John
(d. 1602)

Alexander
(d. 1645)

Richard
(b. 1584)

John
(b. 1589)

Reynold m. Alice ___
(d. 1668–1669) | (d. 1671)

Richard

Oliver

John m. Christian ___
(b. 1619) | (d. 1663)

Richard
(1614–1697?)

William

Olliver m. Margery ___
(d. 1701) | (d. 1715)

Reginald m. twice
(1646–1713)

William
(b. 1685)

Alice
(d. 1707)

Edward m. Amy Kneebone
(d. 1752) | (1677–1756)

Abell m. Sarah Lanyon (?)
(1673–1741)

Edward m. Mary Thomas
(1709–1788) | (1712–1769)

Luce
(1699–1767)

Abell
m. Jane Phillipps
(1701–1767)

Edward m. Mary Rosewarne
(1738–1810) | (1746–1822)

George m. Mary St Aubyn
(d. 1741) | (d. 1743)

Edward m. Catherine Paull
(1779–1842) | (1780–1854)

Thomas m. Henrietta Effield Scudamore
(1817–1885) | (1822–1914)

Edward Scudamore
(1845–1929)
m.
Constance Oldham
1s 3d

Catherine Ann
(1847–1853)

Henrietta Elizabeth
(1850–1878)

William Thomas
(1854–1912)
m.
Emma Carlyon

Catherine Louisa
Harrietta
(1856–1935)
m.
Rev. W. T. Keeling
4s 2d

Margaret Carlyon
m. David JF Warnes
3s 1d

Elizabeth
Carlyon

Barbara Carlyon
m. Gordon T Colbatch
1s 4d

Thomas William Carlyon
(1917–2010)
m. (1) Jean Primrose Sawes 2s 1d
(2) Beverley Robertson Du Rieu 2d

John Carlyon
(1947)
m. Claire Russell Sanderson

Victoria Margaret m. Heath Wesley Amber
(1977)

Richard Russell Carlyon
(1979)
m. Tanya Przbylko

Sophie Elizabeth
(1982)

Emily Claire
(2008)

Henry William Dalmore
(2010)

Thomas Angove (1817–1885), father of Dr William T. Angove

The Angove Family in Cornwall

W hen Dr William Thomas Angove, a Cornish-born medical doctor, emigrated to South Australia in 1886 he had little idea that his wine-making hobby would evolve over the ensuing 125 years into Angove Family Winemakers, one of Australia's largest family-owned and operated wine businesses.

William Angove was born at Mount Pleasant, Camborne, Cornwall on 26 August 1854, the fourth child of Thomas and Henrietta (née Scudamore) Angove. Thomas Angove, like so many others in Cornwall, was associated with the tin and copper mining industry and was the manager of the South Tolcarne Mining Company in Camborne. The family's association with the mining industry went back three generations before Thomas Angove and before that they were yeoman farmers in the parish of Illogan.

The surname Angove from its Cornish origin means 'the smith – an~gove' has been fairly common in Cornwall for more than five centuries. William Thomas Angove's ancestors were farmers at Illogan, north-east of Camborne. His great-grand-father, Edward Angove (1738–1810), was the first recorded member of the family to leave farming to go into the mining industry. By the 1770s he was referred to as Captain Angove, a title that signified he was a mine manager. This was a depressed time in the Cornish mining industry with tin prices down as low as £60 a ton. A later commentator, said that Cornish miners were 'poor beyond the point where poverty remains an incentive to industrious toil.' Not surprisingly, the following century saw huge numbers of Cornish families leave for a new life in North America, New Zealand and Australia.

The financial situation had improved by the time Edward Angove's grandson, Thomas Angove (1817–1885), entered the mining industry, initially working in Ireland and later at Camborne. Whilst in Ireland, Thomas married Henrietta Effield Scudamore, daughter of Lieutenant William James Scudamore R.N. and his wife Catherine Jane (née Hudson) Scudamore, on 19 September 1844. Three children were born while the Angove family was living in Ireland – Edward Scudamore (1845), Catherine Ann (1847) and Henrietta Elizabeth (1850). A further two children were born at Camborne – William Thomas (1854) and Catherine Louisa Harrietta (1856).

The Angove family lived in a two-storey Georgian house at Camborne called Mount Pleasant and Thomas also leased a 58-acre farm near Camborne called Bosprowal, a name that had been in recorded use for 700 years.

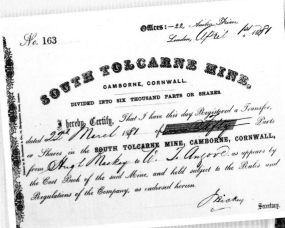

Thomas and Henrietta Angove's house
Mount Pleasant, Cambourne, Cornwall

Bosprowal Farmhouse, Baripper
which was leased by Thomas Angove
from 1870 to 1885

Tregrehan House, near St Austell, home of the Carlyon family; the
name was later used by Thomas W.C. Angove as a wine brand name

Wedding of William T. Angove and Emma Carlyon at Leverington Rectory on 4 September 1879.
William's brother, Dr Edward S. Angove, is at extreme left

Neither of Thomas and Henrietta's sons followed their father into the mining industry but instead both studied medicine at St Bartholomew's Hospital at Smithfield, London. Edward Angove set up in private practice at Camborne and acted as surgeon to several tin mining and smelting works. William Thomas Angove graduated eight years after his elder brother, in 1875. For the first few years he worked in hospitals, including the position of House Physician to the West London Hospital, and gained a reputation for being a 'thoroughly reliable and competent' doctor. Another testimonial, from Dr Alfred Cooper, FRCS, stated that William was 'a kind hearted gentleman, with whom it is very pleasant to work'. In 1878 William became a partner in a private practice at Mildenhall in Suffolk.

During his first year at Mildenhall, Dr Angove met, and subsequently married, Emma Carlyon, daughter of the Rev. Frederick Carlyon of the parish church of St Leonard's, Leverington. The wedding took place at St Leonard's on 4 September 1879. The Carlyons were an old Cornish family, their connections reaching back to Walter Carlyon (d. 1664) of Tregrehan, Parish of St Blazey. His grandson, Thomas Carlyon (d. 1724), built Tregrehan House, near St Austell. The names Carlyon and Tregrehan have continued to be used by the Angove family.

William and Emma Angove had a family of eight children, six of whom survived infancy. The first five were born at Mildenhall – Thomas Carlyon (1880), Hester Scudamore (1881), Lucy (1882), Edward Laurence (1884) and Leonard Michael (1885). William's father died in March 1885 and at much the same time William started the search overseas for a medical practice. Although quite a lot of his letters have survived, in none of them does he give any reason for wanting to make this change. By December 1885 matters were settled regarding a practice at Tea Tree Gully, South Australia, and on 11 March 1886 the family sailed from London on the *Ben Cruachan* destined for South Australia.

Beginnings at Tea Tree Gully

When Dr William Angove took up his new practice (his medical registration is dated 7 July 1886), the village of Tea Tree Gully was the centre of an agricultural district producing livestock, wheat, wool, stone fruits, grapes and apples. The township had a flourmill, two hotels, Wesleyan Chapel and District Council office. William soon found that his practice encompassed a very large area which he variously visited on horseback, carriage and, later, by motor vehicle. He became well-known and respected throughout the district. Three children were born to the Angoves in their first few years at Tea Tree Gully – twins Mary and Harold (1888) and Henrietta Marjorie (1890).

Dr William T. Angove

The rural township of Tea Tree Gully as it was when the Angoves settled there in 1886; the Highercombe Hotel is at centre right

William soon became interested in cereal farming and grape-growing. He leased (and later purchased) 33 acres of land next to his house (this he later named St Agnes Vineyards). In 1891 he purchased 160 acres south-west of Tea Tree Gully, a property called Sarnia Farm. The new vineyards he established were named Tregrehan Vineyards after the Carlyon's property near St Austell, Cornwall.

His interest in winemaking began with the planting of a vineyard on the Tea Tree Gully property and his involvement with the nearby Brightlands wine cellars owned by Archdeacon George Henry Farr. By 1892 William had 10 acres of vines in production and a further 20 acres were planted in 1893 with varieties including Cabernet and Malbec. The vineyard was planted on the square at 9 by 9 foot spacings.

The 1890s saw a rapid increase in vineyard area in southern Australia, largely due to the prospect of a large and stable export market for colonial wines to Great Britain. Planting was fostered by the South Australian Government which gave away millions of vines from its forestry nurseries.

The planting of the Tregrehan Vineyards commenced in 1892 during a period of considerable extension of vine growing in the Tea Tree Gully and Highercombe districts. Vineyard area increased from 165 acres in 1881 to 415 acres in 1896 and 568 acres in 1905. William consulted the State Viticulturist, Professor Arthur J. Perkins, in relation to planting Tregrehan Vineyards. Perkins recommended planting Cabernet Sauvignon (then referred to as Carbenet) on the heavier soils and Malbec on the lighter, well-drained soils. He also planted Mataro, Shiraz, Madeira, Riesling, Gouais and Pineau Blanc.

Tea Tree Gully c. 1900 – Dr Angove's St Agnes Vineyards are to be seen at centre top and Henry Hall's Warboys Vineyards are to the right (north)

The Angove family at home at Tea Tree Gully, c. 1888; photograph by Dr W.T. Angove

The crushing shed at St Agnes which was in use before the cellars were built in 1904–1905 – the must was carted in casks to Brightlands for fermentation; photograph by Dr W.T. Angove

Vintage at St Agnes Cellars, Tea Tree Gully, c. 1905–1910; photograph by Dr W.T. Angove

Brightlands Cellars, Tea Tree Gully, owned by Archdeacon George H. Farr, was where Dr Angove made his first wines (photographed in March 1981)

William Angove continued to make wine at the Brightlands Cellars until he built his own winery on the Tea Tree Gully property in 1904–1905. Archdeacon Farr built the Brightlands Cellars, a two-storied stone building located in a gully just to the north-east of Tea Tree Gully township, in 1875–1976 to process the grapes grown on his property. The cellars were partially underground and maintained an even temperature throughout the year, ideal conditions for the storage of wine.

In the years up to 1905, grapes from the Angove vineyards and from Henry Hall's Warboys Vineyard at Tea Tree Gully were crushed in a shed close to William's house and then the must was carted in hogsheads by horse-drawn trolley to Brightlands to be fermented.

Use of the name St Agnes dates from about 1897. There are a couple of possible reasons as to why William adopted this name. St Agnes is a mining village, 10 miles north-east of Camborne and would have been well-known to the Angove family. Another possible association is with St Agnes, the patron saint of purity, a young Christian who was martyred at Rome in about 350 AD.

The Angove family's long association with wine industry organisations began in 1895 when William was appointed to the Council of the South Australian Vinegrowers' Association (he was a member for 11 years) and the Wine Committee of the Royal Agricultural and Horticultural Society of South Australia. He served as Chairman in 1896 and 1900 and was a judge at the Society's Vine Pruning Competitions.

The earliest extant records of Angove wines are of the 1895 Riesling and White Madeira, both of which were examined by Professor Arthur J. Perkins of Roseworthy Agricultural College and declared to be sound for export. Winemaking at this time was fraught with technical problems, many of which were little understood by winemakers or chemists. William entered his wines in the Royal Agricultural and Horticultural Society Show for the first time in October 1896. He was awarded a Highly Commended Award for his entry in the category *White Wine, 500 gallons, vintage 1895 or older* class, tying with a well-established producer, S. Smith & Sons; first prize went to William Gilbert (Pewsey Vale) and second to Thomas Hardy & Sons. His wines were obviously in good company. The following year, William was awarded Highly Commended for an 1896 Dry Red wine. The judge, W.J. Seabrook, a wine merchant from Melbourne, remarked that 'The very highly commended awards are very good dinner wines'.

The first wine identified by the St Agnes label, the 1897 St Agnes Claret, was certified for export in December 1898. William was also marketing wines under the Tea Tree Gully Vineyard label.

By 1898, William's 18-year-old son Thomas Carlyon Angove was showing an interest in the wine business. Tom (as he was then known, but was later better known as Carl or Skipper Angove) enrolled in the Diploma in Agriculture course at Roseworthy Agricultural College in April 1899. Professor Perkins thought the young student 'will do very well'.

While at Roseworthy Carl befriended Ronald Henry Martin whose family owned Stonyfell Vineyards. The two, who were later to form a business partnership, remained close friends for the rest of their lives. Carl and Ron graduated in 1902; Ron was the College Gold Medallist.

By 1903, the Angove vineyards at Tea Tree Gully amounted to nearly 100 acres and 300 tons of grapes were vintaged that year. Some 10,000 gallons of wine were produced, of which 2000 gallons was a Cabernet Shiraz Dry Red. Most of the wines were dry red or white table wines, with smaller quantities of sweet fortified wines for the local market.

At first the wines were sold locally but when the South Australian Wine & Produce Depot opened in London this became a valuable outlet for Angove wines. At a Commission into the operation of the Depot in 1901, Dr Angove stated: 'I have sent 10,000 gallons of wine [to the Depot], and, although I am in a small way merely, I think the depot has been a Godsend to us. I started marketing wine in a small way and sold locally. I wanted to sell my wine in one lot, and I kept doing so. I do not want to become a retail seller. I think that should be kept separate.

'Some London buyers, who will buy certain quantities, would go round and say, "I will take that cask", and offer a small price that would not pay. Then the depot started, and I sent home all the wine I had. It was some time before I got any returns, and at that time advances were [not] made. Now the returns come in regularly, and I have no trouble in selling. At one time I thought of establishing an agency in the west of England. Mr Young [Manager of the Depot] offered to get me out a label, but thought it would not pay. I took his advice. My sales have averaged 3/3d per gallon. It means about 2/1d net here. That is a very good price for a young wine.

'The bottle trade does not appeal to us in the least. Before the depot, we had great difficulty in selling the wine. Wine has to be two years old before it is fit to go home. There are a large number of vineyards just coming into bearing, and with 2–3 good seasons the cellars will be overflowing again, and everyone will be crying out to get rid of their wine.' When asked if demand currently has overtaken the supply? William replied, 'I am sure of that.'

In June 1904, Tea Tree Gully-born 14-year-old Harold Herbert (Shaver) Beames started to work for Dr Angove; he remained with the family company for 53½ years, finally retiring from the Lyrup Winery, which he had managed for many decades, in 1958.

Late in his life he recalled the occasion when Dr Angove (as he always referred to him) came home one afternoon with some raisin seeds in a packet. These came from a wholesale grocery company in Adelaide where they were used as furnace fuel. The company had developed a way to extract seeds from raisins about which Beames commented, 'It helped small boys, like myself, out of the irksome task of seeding raisins for Christmas puddings.' Dr Angove foresaw another use, as Beames recalled: 'The resultant fermentation showed there was still something to be had from raisin seeds. Plans were laid for a distillery … The distillery began production in 1908. About that time Lexias [Muscat Gordo Blanco] were hard to quit, and many tons of dried fruit forwarded to Sydney failed to find a market, and were returned to the agents at Port Adelaide, stored, and sent to Tea Tree Gully as teams were available, then [fermented and distilled] into spirit.'

This initiative soon led to Carl Angove's decision to establish a distillery in the fruit-growing irrigation settlement at Renmark on the River Murray.

Equipment from Dr Angove's wine laboratory at Tea Tree Gully

Angove & Sons, winemakers and distillers

By 1908, William and Emma's two elder sons, Carl and Edward Laurence (Ted), were assisting their father in the wine business, and in May 1910, the partnership of Angove & Sons was formed. They appointed Roseworthy Agricultural College graduate Arthur Hall as a 'general winery hand'; he went on to become the manager at Tea Tree Gully.

The winemaking enterprise increased rapidly in the period 1904–1910. In 1906 William leased the renowned Highercombe Vineyard at Highercombe. The 45-acre vineyard was located in the cooler hills to the south-east of Tea Tree Gully. Carl admired the lighter European styles of dry wines and recognised that such styles could be grown at Highercombe. They leased Highercombe until the vintage of 1913–1914, which owing to unprecedented storms during October 1913 was the worst season they had experienced.

William appointed his first distributor, W.F. Roberts & Co. of Adelaide, in 1906. The list of wines on offer included Ingleberg Hock and St Agnes Special Vintage Claret; it was 'stimulating and recommended by experts for Invalids'. With the expansion of the export market, William established a depot and office at Port Adelaide in 1908.

A distillery was established in 1908 at St Agnes and the distillery building soon became a well-known feature in the landscape at Tea Tree Gully. The distillery was capable of handling up to 300,000 gallons of wine a year. A report in September 1910 stated that the distillery equipment included a 700-gallon pot still and a 500-gallon rectifying still. During that year, the company was taking surplus raisins from Renmark and was distilling the wine produced using the dried fruit.

In 1910 Angove & Sons started to prepare a further 50 acres for planting, and the following year they leased a 74-acre vineyard on Tolley Road owned by St Peter's College (Adelaide); this vineyard became known as The College Block and they continued to lease it for the next 60 years.

Winemaking and medicine were just two of Dr Angove's varied interests. He was a man of great natural curiosity and seemingly boundless energy. His other interests, or hobbies, included photography, geology, ornithology, lepidoptry (butterflies), sailing, fishing, golf, shooting and matters mechanical. He was a member of the Loyal Highercombe Lodge and a Justice of the Peace. Emma was left to care for the house and family. She was reputed to have complained that 'he treated his patients but never sent out any accounts'.

Silver trophy awarded to Dr Angove on 13 January 1900 by The Adelaide Sailing Club for his 18 ft Class Boat, Redwing

Emma Angove
(née Carlyon)

Dr William T. Angove

Light St. Agnes Sherry.
TRADE MARK
Angove & Sons
SOUTH AUSTRALIAN WINE   REGISTERED.

St. Agnes Vineyards,

TEA TREE GULLY,

SOUTH AUSTRALIA.

	Per Dozen Quarts.	Per Dozen Pints.	Per Dozen Hf Pts.	Per Gallon.
Clarets.				
St. Agnes Claret (light)	...			
Gold Label Claret	...			
Special Light Claret	...			
White Wines.				
Riesling	...			
Chablis	...			
Hock	...			
Hock, Ingleberg	...			
Ports and Sherries				
► Fine Old Medicinal Port	...			
Fine Old Vintage Port	...			
Old Port	...			
Fine Old Sweet Sherries (Ladies' Wine)				
Frontignac	...			
Domestic Wines.				
White Sweet	...			
White No. 1 Sweet	...			
Fine Old Sweet White	...			
Red, Sweet (Hermitage)	...			
Red, No 1 Sweet	...			
Fine Old Sweet Red	...			

All Prices include Bottles, Packing, and Cases.

Wines at per gallon do not de Flagons.

llowed on empty returns if ood order.

St. Agnes Claret

DR. ANGOVE'S
SOUTH AUSTRALIAN
WINES
Guaranteed Pure & Unadulterated.

St. Agnes Special Vintage Claret is stimulating and recommended by experts for Invalids.

Cellars TEA TREE GULLY.
Depot 7? PIRIE ST. ADELAID

Adelaide Manager   W. F. ROBERTS

August 14th 1908

Price-List Dr. Angove's Wines and

	Per Doz. Quarts.	Per Doz. Pints.	
St. Agnes Claret (Special Vintage)	12/-	7/-	4/-
St. Agnes Claret (Light)			4/6
Fine O.V. Port	15/-		
Old Port	12/-	7/-	4/-
Reisling			
Hock Ingleberg (Special)			
Hock			
Sweet White			
Sweet Red	15/-		4/6
Fine Old Sherry	15/-		4/6
Fine Old Sherry (Sweet)			

The St. Agnes Wines are carefully made, and well matured before they leave the Cellars. The most up-to-date methods are practised, and the business is such that personal supervision in every branch is possible, thus a reliable article is produced.

TELEPHONE—"ANGOVE, TEA TREE GULLY."

ST. AGNES WINES.
TRADE MARK.

Special . . . .
Christmas
Price List.

Vineyards and Cellars TEA TREE GULLY.

W. T. ANGOVE,
PROPRIETOR.

J. H. Sneering & Co., Printers, Adelaide.

William was a well-respected bird observer, collector and member of the South Australian Ornithological Association. Edward (Ted) Angove's widow, Dorothy, donated his collection to the Association in December 1921. It passed to the South Australian Museum in 1932. Photography was an adjunct to his interest in birds and he photographed birds and their nests, as well as many other subjects. William's interest in the natural world gave him a wider appreciation of the interaction between animals and their habitat. To this end he retained areas of native bush on his properties. These areas still survive and the largest area is now Angove Conservation Park, so named in his honour.

For many residents at Tea Tree Gully, William gave them their first experience of a motor vehicle. He became a familiar sight going on his visits on his mechanised bicycle and later a succession of motorcars – a White Steamer, 6 h.p. Humberette and 8 h.p. De Dion Bouton. On one occasion, his motorcar collided with a horse and buggy. The ladies affected were taken to a nearby house where Dr Angove duly attended them!

In 1907 William purchased a 10 h.p. De Dion Bouton and Carl a Clement Talbot. The De Dion had the registration number of 77. This was the first of a succession of vehicles to have this number. Carl inherited his father's liking for De Dions. His best remembered vehicle was a 1925 De Dion which was affectionately known as 'The White Lady'. Carl later imported from England a very smart blue and yellow Standard Swallow Mk 1. Not all of his means of transport were as fast as the Standard Swallow. In the early years of travelling to and from Renmark he rode a Triumph pedal-assisted motorcycle.

William and Emma Angove visited Great Britain in 1909 and called on various family members. It is likely that it was on this visit that William was diagnosed with a malignant growth in his throat. They returned to Adelaide, travelled in New South Wales and then attended Carl's marriage to Margaret Bessie Fletcher, daughter of William Fletcher of Semaphore, at St Bede's Church, Semaphore, on 25 April 1911. Although the Fletcher family was involved with shipping, they could claim an earlier connection with the wine industry as William Fletcher's wife, Margaret Bessie, was a daughter of the pioneer winemaker and writer Dr Alexander Charles Kelly. Dr Kelly was a major shareholder in the Tintara Vineyard Company at McLaren Vale.

In mid-1911 William Angove returned to Great Britain and spent the last months of his life at the home of his brother, Dr Edward Angove. William died at *The Hermitage*, Silverdale, Lancashire on 25 March 1912 aged 58 years.

T.C. Angove married Margaret Bessie Fletcher on 25 April 1911

Edward Angove changing a tyre on his father's 10 h.p. De Dion Bouton – registration number 77 – purchased in 1907; photograph by Dr W.T. Angove

The move to Renmark

In 1910 Angove & Sons became the first company to establish a winery and distillery on the River Murray in South Australia.

The brothers George and William B. Chaffey developed an irrigation settlement at Renmark, commencing in 1887. The Chaffeys had developed irrigation settlements in California before being enticed to come to Australia by Alfred Deakin to undertake such a development in Victoria. Delays in getting the approvals to develop Mildura Station led to an offer from the South Australian Government to establish a fruit colony at Bookmark Station, soon to become known as Renmark. The early years of the colony were difficult as they coincided with the economic depression of the early 1890s but by 1910 the area was producing large quantities of stone and citrus fruits and grapes. Markets for the produce were being sought.

In the vintages of 1909 and 1910, William Angove purchased both fresh and dried grapes from Renmark for processing into spirit at Tea Tree Gully. Some 400 tons of Lexias (Muscat Gordo Blanco) were transported to Tea Tree Gully for processing in 1909. This was a major undertaking for the time. A natural progression was to process the fruit at Renmark and Carl Angove made an offer to the Australian Dried Fruits' Association to build a distillery at Renmark. Construction began on 12 December 1910.

Construction of an irrigation channel at Renmark in 1889; photograph by Ernest Gall

River transport P.S. Queen at Renmark,
c. 1900–1909

Thomas (T.C.) Angove – later known as Carl – boiling
the billy on the road to Renmark. The motor vehicle
is his father's 10 h.p. DeDion Bouton, purchased in
1907, the first of many Angove motor cars to have
the registration number 77.

Angove's Renmark
Distillery, c. 1912–1915

Angove's Renmark Distillery, c. 1912–1915

Pencil and charcoal sketch
of T.C. (Skipper) Angove

Wood storage at the
Renmark Distillery, c. 1917

Lieut. Edward Lawrence Angove,
10th Australian Infantry Battalion

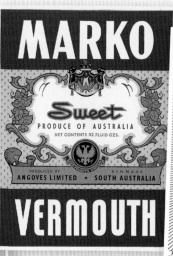
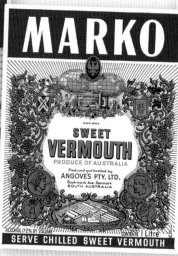
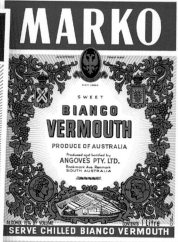
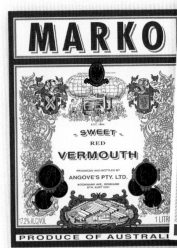
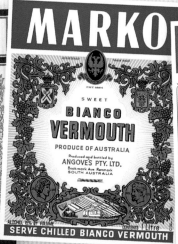
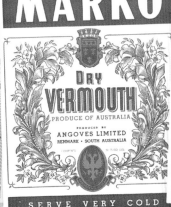
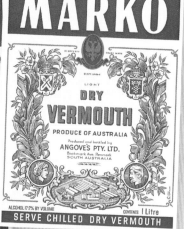
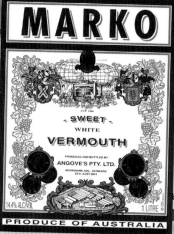
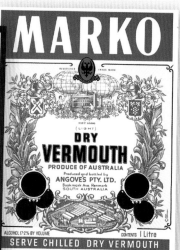

Development of the Marko Vermouth label

The distillery was operational in time for the 1911 vintage when 200 tons of dried fruit and 300 tons of fresh Muscat Gordo were processed, paying up to £4/12/6 per ton. A report at the time said there was good scope for planting Doradillo, Gouais and Grenache for distillation. The winery had a storage capacity of 70,000 gallons and 20,000 proof gallons of brandy or spirit was made that year.

Shaver Beames moved to Renmark at this time and years later recalled that dried fruit was brought to the winery direct from the drying greens, mostly in wooden trays. 'This was beautiful fruit but no one wanted it. Still, it's not my purpose to tell you of the low state of the dried fruit market at the time, beyond repeating the words of one of Renmark's oldest growers who carted Gordos to Angove's winery right from the start; words spoken to me just over a year ago, "It was a godsend Angoves coming to Renmark – it saved Renmark."'

The Lyrup Wine Co. winery, 1938

Extensions continued to the business with the development of a winery at the Lyrup Village Settlement and the purchase of a share in a fruit-packing business. The Lyrup Wine Company (formed January 1914) was a joint enterprise of Carl Angove and Ron Martin. Although Lyrup was located just 11 km west of Renmark, there was no way to cross the River Murray and it made sense to process fruit at Lyrup. The new winery was completed in time for the 1914 vintage and 30,000 gallons of wine were produced. This was probably the first beverage (table) wine produced in the Riverland of South Australia. By 1917 production had risen to 268 tons of fruit yielding 50,000 gallons of wine. Shaver Beames managed Lyrup Winery from its foundation until he retired in 1958. His forte as a winemaker was the production of fortified wines and vermouths; the latter laid the foundations of Angove's famous Marko vermouths. Wine production continued at Lyrup Winery until 1977.

In March 1913 Carl Angove acquired a share in the fruit-packing business of Cole & Woodham of Renmark. A house near the packing sheds in Tarcoola Street was the company's office and from 1922 became the office for all of the Angove operations. In January 1915 Thomas Foggo Whillas was appointed company secretary. He retained this role until his retirement in 1950 and for much of that time was Carl Angove's right-hand man.

The Angove family moved to live at Renmark in 1913 and built *Cultara* off the Paringa Road on the bank of what was then the main channel of the River Murray. Their eldest child, Margaret Carlyon, was born while they were still living at North Adelaide, in 1912. Their other children were Elizabeth Carlyon (1913), Barbara Carlyon (1914) and Thomas William Carlyon (1917). *Cultara* remained the family's home until 1923 when they moved to Glenelg to be nearer to the children's schools.

While Carl was establishing the distillery at Renmark, the operations at Tea Tree Gully were under the direction of his brother Ted and Arthur Hall. Both Ted and Len (known as Mick) Angove enlisted for service during World War I. Len served in the 27th Battalion and Ted in the 10th Australian Infantry Battalion. Ted was killed in action in the second Battle of the Somme on 23 August 1918. Following his discharge, Len took up a fruit block at Renmark but later became a maintenance engineer at the Renmark Distillery before moving to Sydney.

Skipper and Margaret Angove's first home at Renmark – Cultara on the Paringa Road – during the 1917 flood

A period of expansion

5

As the production of grapes increased in the Riverland (as the district eventually became known) more wineries were established. The Adelaide Wine Company (Chateau Tanunda) established at Renmark in 1914 but by 1916 was in financial difficulties. Carl Angove purchased the company's stock of wine and the premises were taken over by the newly formed Renmark Growers' Co-operative Winery and Distillery. A second co-operative winery was established in 1922, at Berri. The only other private winery to be established in the Riverland in this period was Thomas Hardy & Sons, at Waikerie in 1915; this was sold to local growers in 1919 and became Waikerie Co-operative Distillery Company. As early as 1923 Carl Angove could see a sound future for grape-growing in the Riverland, as he wrote, 'The first steps to success were to plant the better kinds of vines and to let the grapes mature properly. If they do this they will at any rate be on the right road, and I think, the industry will come out all right.'

Delivering grapes to the Renmark Distillery, 1927

The transport of goods to and from the Riverland was an impediment to the growing business. For the first few years all goods were moved by paddle steamer. Wine, along with dried and fresh fruit, was loaded at Renmark Wharf (also at Lyrup) and taken by paddle steamer to Morgan where it was transferred to rail for the trip to Adelaide. After 1913 Angove used the new railway extension to Paringa; casks of wine were taken from Renmark Wharf to Paringa by barges. The railway extension to Renmark was delayed by the war and post-war financial constraints and was not completed until 1927.

In spite of the transport difficulties, the company did well financially at Renmark, and by 1919 it was returning a healthy annual profit. Angove & Sons had borrowed a considerable sum of money to establish the winery and distillery at Renmark but their assets at Renmark and Tea Tree Gully, as valued by John G. Kelly, were worth £22,000. Carl Angove would have felt that the future for the company was looking good.

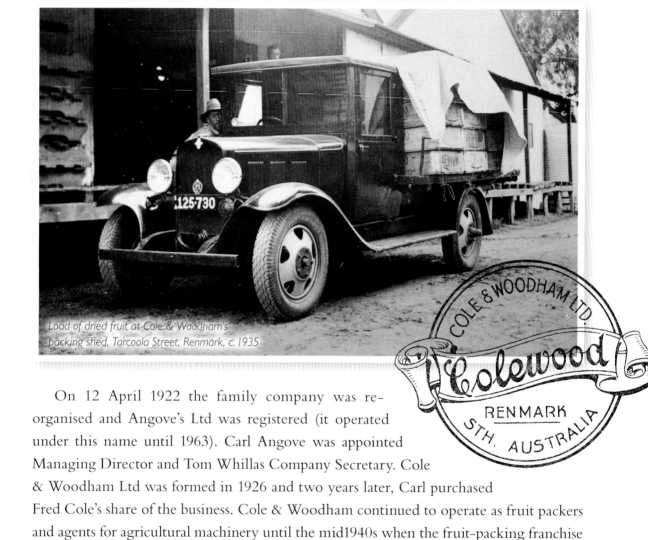

Load of dried fruit at Cole & Woodham's packing shed, Tarcoola Street, Renmark, c. 1935.

On 12 April 1922 the family company was re-organised and Angove's Ltd was registered (it operated under this name until 1963). Carl Angove was appointed Managing Director and Tom Whillas Company Secretary. Cole & Woodham Ltd was formed in 1926 and two years later, Carl purchased Fred Cole's share of the business. Cole & Woodham continued to operate as fruit packers and agents for agricultural machinery until the mid1940s when the fruit-packing franchise was sold. The business then moved to new premises in 14th Street, Renmark.

The wine business continued to grow. By 1927 Angove's Ltd had 190 acres of vineyards at Tea Tree Gully; the plantings included Doradillo (101 acres – used for distillation and fortified wines), Mataro (24), Cabernet Sauvignon (26) and Shiraz (15). The St Agnes Cellars had fermentation capacity of 34,800 gallons and storage for 117,700 gallons, a quarter of which was in wood. The Renmark winery had a fermentation capacity of 47,500 gallons and storage for 34,365 gallons in wood and 259,000 gallons in concrete tanks.

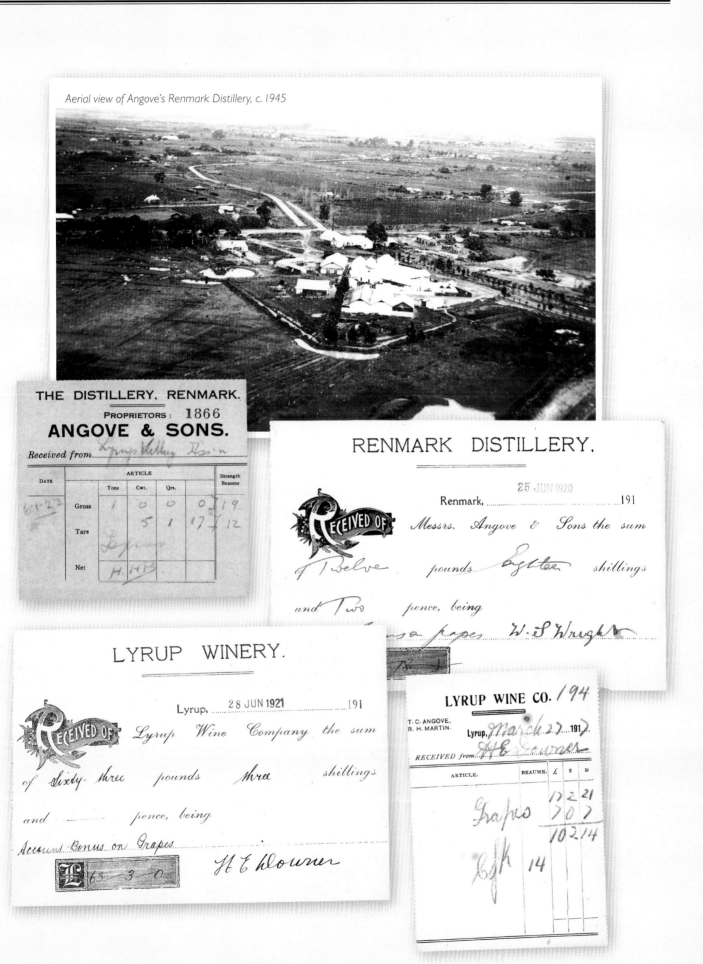

Aerial view of Angove's Renmark Distillery, c. 1945

THE DISTILLERY, RENMARK.

PROPRIETORS : **1866**

ANGOVE & SONS.

Received from

DATE	ARTICLE			Strength Beaume
	Tons	Cwt.	Qrs.	
Gross	1	0	0	0 19
Tare		5	1	17 12
Net	H.413.			

RENMARK DISTILLERY.

Renmark, ...191

RECEIVED OF *Messrs. Angove & Sons the sum*

of Twelve pounds *Eighteen* shillings

and Two pence, being

.... W. S. Wright

LYRUP WINERY.

Lyrup, 28 JUN 1921 191

RECEIVED OF *Lyrup Wine Company the sum*

of Sixty-three pounds *three* shillings

and ———— pence, being

Account Bonus on Grapes

H. E. Downer

63 3 0

LYRUP WINE CO. 194

T. C. ANGOVE,
R. H. MARTIN.

Lyrup, March 27 191

RECEIVED from

ARTICLE.	BEAUME	£	S	D
Grapes		12	2	21
		70	7	
		10	2	14
	14			

STAGNES

Loads of St Agnes Brandy leaving the Renmark Distillery, c. 1936

Development of St Agnes Brandy

Roseworthy graduates Ron Haselgrove and John Guinand joined Angove in 1925. Both men worked closely with Carl Angove, Ron in winemaking and distilling and John took charge of sales and spent much of his time promoting Angove products both interstate and overseas. Ron remained with Angove until March 1938 and, early in the period, he was involved with Carl Angove in the development of St Agnes Brandy, a brand that soon became a household name throughout Australia. Their aim was to produce a lighter, more delicate style of brandy than had previously been produced in Australia. They developed a delicate Pot Still brandy, double distilled after the method used in Cognac.

It is generally believed that the original St Agnes brandy label was designed by Carl's eldest daughter, Margaret, and the drawing of the winery used on it was by John C. Goodchild, a personal friend of the Angove family. It was based on an aerial photograph of the St Agnes winery taken from a 'box kite'. According to Tom Angove, 'The label in this form was first used in the early 1930s. Its appearance hasn't changed appreciably over the years, however, the original being dark in visage having a good deal of black in it with the green giving it dark shadows compared to the much lighter colour of the present form. The label design was registered on 21 June 1934. The figure of St Agnes was added to the design in October 1963.'

St Agnes Brandy soon became an established name in the market place and gained show awards in both Australia and Europe. The range was expanded with the introduction of St Agnes Old Liqueur Brandy in 1942 and St Agnes Very Old (or XO) in 1965.

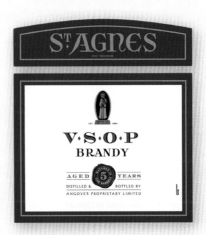

Evolution of St Agnes label, 1934 to the present

As at 2011, Collotype Printers in Adelaide have printed every St Agnes Brandy label ever produced. Collotype were fine art printers prior to a visit from T.C. Angove who enquired whether they would be able to produce St Agnes Brandy labels for the company. Today Collotype is one of the leading wine and spirit label printers in the world.

Wine exports

Although Angove had been exporting wine to Great Britain since the 1890s, it was not until the 1920s that conditions favoured a substantial increase in exports to Great Britain and South-East Asia. In 1924 the Commonwealth Government passed the Wine Export Bounty Act. This applied to wine exported to Great Britain which contained not less than 34% proof spirit and covered all sweet wines fortified with grape spirit. The bounty, initially, amounted to 2/9d per gallon. However, without additional tariff concessions from Great Britain, the cost of Australian wines on arrival was still significantly higher than those imported from Europe. In the 1925 budget the British Government introduced a new system of Imperial Preference for all goods and produce from British Empire countries. The combined effect of the wine bounty and the new tariff arrangements encouraged wine exports and Australia's overseas exports of wine exceeded 1 million gallons for the first time in 1925–1926 and reached 3.7 million gallons in 1927–1928. The export demand was no longer for dry red wines but for sweet fortified styles. This was especially advantageous to the wineries on the River Murray.

T.C. (Skipper) Angove, Royal South Australian Yacht Club Squadron Commodore from 1931 to 1938

The wine bounty was extended beyond its expiry date of 31 August 1927, although the rate was reduced from 4/- per gallon to 3/-. It remained in place until February 1940 but the rate per gallon continued to decline. Imperial Preference was also maintained and had a significant effect on the importation of Australian wines and brandy into Great Britain and Empire countries. A number of the larger family-owned wineries in South Australia, including Angove, were in a good position to take advantage of the situation and they were financially rewarding years for the companies.

Carl Angove went to Great Britain in 1927 to investigate the feasibility of establishing an agency for Angove wines in London. As a result, Dominion Wines Ltd was established in October 1929 (as wine importers), a partnership between Carl and Ron Martin. A second company,

Dominion Wines (Distributors) Ltd, was established as wholesalers for Angove and Stonyfell wines; this company was later succeeded by Margoves Ltd. Great Britain was to become an important market for Angove wines for the next two decades during which time they were one of the top four Australian wine companies exporting to Great Britain. Carl and Ron's association also extended to industry bodies as both served on the Council of the South Australian Vinegrowers' Association and The Federal Viticultural Council of Australia.

Wine was not Carl's only passion in life. As with his father, Carl had a lifetime interest in motorcars, boating and sailing. The latter interests gave Carl his nickname 'Skipper' Angove. His best-remembered craft was the 17 metre auxiliary yacht *Stormy Petrel* that he bought in association with Ron Martin and Tom Crompton. Skipper Angove was a member of the Royal South Australian Yacht Squadron and was Commodore from 1931 to 1938. He was also a member of the Royal Australian Naval Volunteer Reserve; he was promoted to the rank of Lieutenant in 1932. Each year the RSAYS held a race from Outer Harbour to Kangaroo Island and back. *Stormy Petrel* was the fastest yacht on the run. Sadly, the beautiful yacht was wrecked off the north coast of Kangaroo Island in December 1937.

Aboard the Stormy Petrel –
*L to R: Tom Hardy, Skipper Angove
and Ron Martin*

*'A' Class boats racing on St Vincent Gulf
on 13 December 1930. L to R:* Nautilus,
Anyandah, Noralli *and* Stormy Petrel

*St Agnes Winery and Distillery,
c. 1925 – the dam was built in
1924 to provide the winery with
a more reliable water supply*

Consolidation at St Agnes Winery

By the time the decision to develop a winery at Renmark was made in 1910, the St Agnes winery and vineyards were well-established. Following Ted Angove's death, the management at St Agnes passed to Arthur Hall. He remained as manager for the next 28 years. The employees included a number of men who had started during Dr Angove's time – cellar foreman Jim Phillips, vineyard foreman Jim Lambert and vineyard overseer Joe (Giuseppe) Paoli from whom many of the men learnt the art of pruning.

Arthur Hall's son Dennis recalled his father's tasks at St Agnes: 'ACH's duty was to organise and supervise all work at the cellars and in the vineyards. He kept the books, answered correspondence, and directed the work of the place. An excise officer attended two or three days a week, and ACH had to use those times to ensure that wines which would be likely to be needed for sales blends were released from bond.'

Regarding Carl Angove, he remarked: 'He ran his Cellars like a ship and in rare slack periods cellar hands would be busy scraping and painting. When a man or boy could be spared from the vineyard he would be brought in to chip grass, trim trees and generally tidy the premises.

'When you entered the main gate to the cellars you couldn't help being impressed by the neatness. There was a sense of stability and order about the wide entrance yard and the white-washed walls of the fermenting house and spirit bond.

'He and ACH seemed always to work closely, easily and without friction. The whole place ran with remarkable smoothness. T.C. [Carl Angove] knew exactly what he wanted. He left it to ACH to put his intentions into action.'

A now largely forgotten practice was the use of a sealant over the concrete floors. This not only made the floors look good but it enabled the winery to be kept cleaner than was possible with a concrete surface. Arthur Hall recorded: 'Floor Stain – 11 lb Johnson [sic Johnstone] & Nicholls English Burnt Sienna to 3 gals raw linseed oil – mix Sienna to smooth paste then add oil (3 coats).' Sienna is a form of limonite clay and as a pigment gives the paint a deep red-brown colour.

The vineyards were worked using horses well into the 1930s. Carl Angove was proud of their draught horses. He once stated that he would not put a tractor on his vineyards until the horses became too old to work. It very nearly happened that way; for some years the company had horses and tractors working side by side in their vineyards. The vine rows were ploughed using horses and then hand-hoed for follow-up weed control. Spraying was also done by hand. Arthur Hall recorded in his diary that spraying the 210 acres of vineyards with bluestone and lime with one machine took three men 15 days – they covered 14 acres per day.

Aerial view of St Agnes Winery and Distillery, c. 1932

Angove had many long-serving employees during their 125 years of operations at Tea Tree Gully. Men who joined the company prior to the late 1940s included Jack Lambert (c. 1895–1938), Arthur Hall (1910–1946), W.S. (Bill) Hockey (1912–1973), Perce Goodes (1917–1967), Charlie Neale (c. 1922–1956), Max Steinwedel (1926–1979), Jim Rawlings (1926–1973), Gladstone Jackson (1927–1957), Ern Lokan (1932–1965), Tim Steinwedel (1937–1979), Bob Lokan (1942–1964) and Ray Goodes (1944–1984).

Bill Hockey worked for Angove for a record number of years. He was just 14 when he began working for the company and he spent most of his career in the vineyard. He lost his hearing as a result of an illness when he was in his teens but he learnt to lip-read and could carry on a 'normal conversation' with great ease. Ray Goodes described Bill as a 'terrific bloke'. He recalled, 'The men would be sitting around at morning smoko talking about the weekend and Bill would be involved in all the various conversations. His eyes were so alert and he was an excellent lip-reader.'

Five years after Bill joined Angove, 15-year-old Perce Goodes was employed as a vineyard hand. In his early years with the company, Perce carted grapes from the Highercombe Vineyard to St Agnes Cellars. Driving a dray loaded with grapes and two horses down the steep Anstey's Hill Road to the winery was an experience he never forgot. Perce remained with Angove for all his working life, except for brief periods during the Depression when most of the men were only fully employed during vintage and pruning times. During these lay-off periods he went well sinking.

By the early 1930s wine styles were beginning to change. Sweet fortified wines and dry red clarets were still produced, but new and substantial effort was made to

Bill Hockey spent his early years with Angove working at the renowned Highercombe Vineyards. He later recalled: 'Only the grapes from the Highercombe vineyards were crushed at the Highercombe Cellars. I picked grapes, pruned in the vineyards and worked in the cellars. Shiraz and Rhine Riesling were the only grapes grown at Highercombe. The vineyards were very good plantings but a little on the hard side to work as they were on the hillside.' Bill was runner-up in the local pruning championships in 1924 and 1928 and outright winner in 1929 and 1930. Bill was a meticulous pruner and many of the later vineyard men learnt from him.

improve the dry sherries. A new storage cellar for sherry hogsheads was built and the foundations were laid for what eventually became Angove's Fino Dry Flor Sherry. At much the same time, the pot still was dismantled and taken to Renmark. Of the sherries, Dennis Hall wrote: 'Angove made at Tea Tree Gully very fine dry sherries, wines with a lot of character and vinosity but without coarseness, the sort of sherries I think of as "English sherries" … The platitudinous Australian sweet sherry had no place in the interests and affection of Carl Angove and Arthur Hall.' Arthur Hall's other favourite wines were the Tea Tree Gully vintage ports, of which he considered the 1923 and 1940 to be outstanding.

Arthur kept the clean juice (free-run) separate from the pressings and when necessary, lowered the Beaume by the addition of water. Milk was used to fine the wine (20 gallons in 900 gallons of wine). In the 1934 vintage he recorded processing Grenache, White Grenache, Mataro, Doradillo and Pedro grapes. Regarding Mataro, he wrote, 'Generally a mad ferment, look out for temperature & consequent [need] for extra sulphur. Add 4 oz tannin per 100 [gallons]

Arthur Hall's meticulously kept notebook gives a picture of winemaking in the 1920s and 1930s, a period from which relatively little practical detail has come down to us. He was using sulphur in the wines, a significant factor at a time when wine diseases were commonplace. In March 1921 he noted, 'Running off Greenache [Grenache] – 5 oz to 100 gals of BiSulphite.' Also, 'Hock – run juice straight off 10½ to 11 B [Beaume] – add 1½ lbs citric acid + 2 oz sulphur [to 100 gallons]. Stand 24 hours rack & add 2 ozs tannin.'

when taken off skins.' For Doras [Doradillo] he says, 'Definitely add acid to all Doras but check as each vintage may take a varying amount; spread over vat in layers if the wine is to be fermented on skins.' It was a practical approach, essentially learning on the job.

Lokan Bros of Modbury carting export hogsheads of wine for Angove's Ltd from the winery to Port Adelaide, 1925

Flor sherry grew in importance in the 1930s. Making a good Flor sherry was an exacting matter. In 1939 Arthur Hall recorded: 'If acidity fairly high do not add, as Flor grows best with low acidity. Add usual amounts of tannin 12 oz T pure to 100 gals & bisulphite 6 oz per 100 gals provided the Flor Culture is acclimatised to 6 oz. Add Culture which can be fermented in the flasks. Seed the Flor in Hhds from Flor kept growing in the office by using a pipette & add gently on top of the wine. The Flor sinks to the bottom very easily. Watch growth & do not disturb unless necessary for microscopic [examination] purposes.'

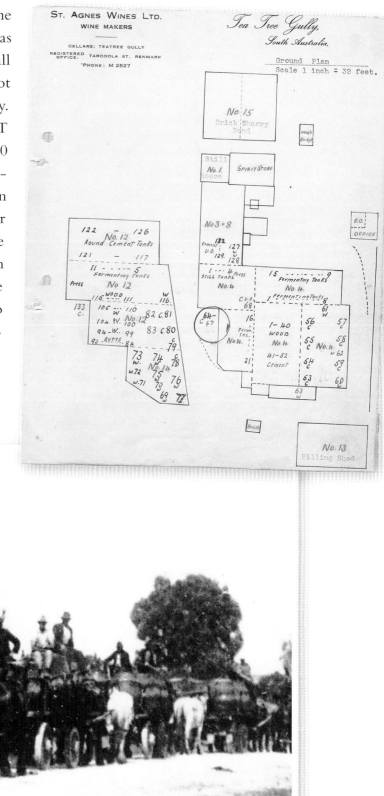

The next generation

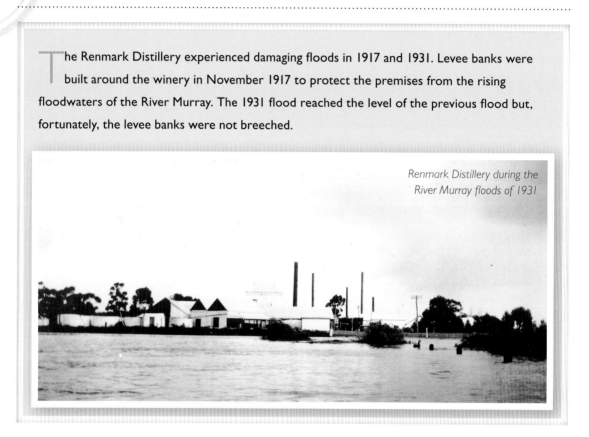

The Renmark Distillery experienced damaging floods in 1917 and 1931. Levee banks were built around the winery in November 1917 to protect the premises from the rising floodwaters of the River Murray. The 1931 flood reached the level of the previous flood but, fortunately, the levee banks were not breeched.

Renmark Distillery during the River Murray floods of 1931

By the mid-1940s the next generation of the Angove family, Tom Angove, was completing his education in preparation for an active role in the company. Tom Angove recalled that he did not like school very much until he discovered physics and chemistry. His academic leanings lead him to enrol in the Diploma in Agriculture course at Roseworthy Agricultural College in 1936. At the end of second year he transferred to the Oenology course (introduced in 1936, the first of its type in Australia). Tom graduated R.D.Oe. in March 1940 and was awarded the Gold Medal, given by Leo Buring for the highest aggregate in all diploma subjects, the prize for individual study (project) presented by Karl Weidenhofer, and the tasting prize given by R.H. Martin. Tom's individual project was on modified distillery procedure.

At much the same time as Tom completed his studies at Roseworthy his parents sold their home at Glenelg and returned to live at Renmark. They built a two-storey house, elevated off the ground on the banks of the River Murray in Renmark. Margaret Angove designed *Terragong* (as it was later named by Tom, an Aboriginal word meaning *dry land*

and water) and she supervised the construction from the Renmark Hotel where they lived for the duration. Tom recalled, 'Mater supervised the building down to where the screws should go. She worked from a writing pad of notes and details. Mater knew exactly what she wanted.'

In February 1941 Tom Angove became a director of Angove's Ltd along with his father and Tom Whillas. On 12 September 1941 he joined the Royal Australian Air Force (RAAF) as a trainee pilot. On the completion of training (as Flying Officer 409490) he went to Rathmines for conversion to water-borne craft. He was then stationed at various operational bases in the South-West Pacific. He was discharged from the RAAF in September 1944. Tom subsequently joined the Renmark Branch of the Returned Soldiers' (later Services') League.

Tom married Jean Primrose Sawers in the Chapel of St Peter's College, Adelaide, on 10 February 1942. Tom and Jean had three children – Jeanette Primrose (Jenny), David Carlyon and John Carlyon; they divorced in 1953. When Tom's mother, Margaret, moved from *Terragong* to live at North Adelaide, Tom and his family moved into the family home at Renmark. On 7 August 1958, Tom married Beverley (Bib) Robertson DuRieu; they had two daughters, Frances Beverley and Sarah Kathleen.

The war years

During Tom's absence from Renmark during the war years, the management of the family business reverted to his father. Carl was supported during this period by a capable group of men, including William (Bill) J. Marshall who was in charge of distillation, and Tom Whillas and Cyril Brady in the company office. War-time constraints of depleted staff, rationing and shortages of all types took a toll of Carl's health. The winery office was moved to temporary accommodation at the winery in 1941 and the new offices were built in 1943–1944. Carl's interest in woodworking gave rise to the use of natural timber in partitioning walls; these remain a distinctive feature of the building.

On his return from active service in September 1944, Tom assumed a greater role in the management of the Angove companies. He became a director of St Agnes Wines and Lyrup Wine Company in 1945 with his father and Ron Martin. Carl Angove retired as Managing Director of Angove's Ltd on 28 November 1946 and was succeeded by his son. The directors of the company were Carl Angove, Tom Angove, Tom Whillas and John Guinand. Carl was also a partner with Ron Martin in a Victorian-based firm of wine distributors, Oakley Adams Ltd. (The Angove-Martin partnerships in St Agnes Wines Ltd and Lyrup Wine Co. Ltd were dissolved in 1950 and 1953 respectively, and in February 1954 Angove's Ltd acquired the shares of H.M. Martin & Sons in Dominion Wines.)

The company's intake of grapes had been gradually increasing and the 1945 vintage was the largest Angove had processed, some 2954 tons, 2175 at Renmark, 407 tons at Lyrup and 372 tons at Tea Tree Gully. A total of 521,237 gallons of wine were produced.

During 1946 Tom Angove designed and built a large vintage house at Renmark. It has 32 open fermenters each of 10 tons capacity, eight closed fermenters of 30 tons capacity, 10 underground tanks each of 2250 gallons capacity, eight high tanks each of 3200 gallons capacity, three grape crushers with hoppers and elevators, two twin-screw presses and associated equipment. It was designed to handle 7000 tons of grapes in a vintage, which it did and considerably more under pressure before further extensions were made.

In the post-War years, Robert Hill became chief winemaker, David Whillas became head chemist, and Robert (Bob) Abbott was appointed secretary of Cole & Woodham,

Inside the vintage house built in 1946 – designed by Tom Angove

Aerial view of Angove's Renmark Distillery, September 1951

Angove offices, Renmark – watercolour painting by John C. Goodchild

and two years later (November 1952) became acting-secretary of Angove's Ltd. John Guinand became sales manager in 1946 and undertook many promotional trips interstate and overseas, particularly to South-East Asia.

Carl Angove, who had been in indifferent health for some years, died at his Renmark home in on 24 January 1952 aged 72 years.

W.F.H. Edmonds, President of the Upper Murray Grapegrowers' Association, paid tribute to Skipper Angove:

'With the passing of T.C. Angove there steps down from the ranks of the River pioneers, the man with the faith and determination in the potentialities of the River areas in the establishment of the wine industry. …To such a man we owe much, for his leadership, his knowledge, his faith and courage in a belief, clarity of purpose and dignity in execution.'

Installing the new boiler, October 1951

A.V. (Bert) Nightingale with one of his charges, 1956

Mr T.W.C. Angove
Renmark, South Australia.

Grape delivery at Renmark Distillery, mid 1950s

The Angove Coat-of-Arms

Dr William T. Angove registered a trademark for his wine business in 1908. It comprised a double-headed eagle with wings and legs outspread. Its origin is not known with certainty, but prior to this, in January 1883, in a letter to his brother Edward, he wrote, 'Will you send me one of the crests you had done: say how you found out all about it.' Dr Edward Angove's reply to this question has not survived but Dr Angove's grandson, Tom Angove, possessed a gold cygnet ring that belonged to Dr Edward Angove bearing the eagle crest. Tom inherited it from Dr Edward's granddaughter by marriage, Mrs Kate Garbett, in 1961.

Prior to this, in 1948, T.C. Angove approached the College of Arms, London with regard to registering the Armorial Seal – a spread double-headed eagle – from the Angove Coat-of-Arms as a trademark. Investigations by the College of Arms found that the arms were those of Abell/Abel Angove (1673–1741), of the Parish of Illogan. However, the College of Arms had no extant Arms for the name of Angove and suspect that the Arms being investigated may never have been officially recorded.

The outcome of the searches was that the College of Arms was unwilling to confirm the supposed Angove Arms, but were prepared to incorporate the principal feature, the double-headed eagle, slightly modified, in a new granting of Arms. The new shield depicts the family interests of mining and winemaking, with a motto of *Deo Volente Vincam*, God willing, I shall conquer.

T.C. Angove died before the Coat of Arms was granted, so when the grant was made on 20 May 1953 it was to his son, T.W.C. Angove. Soon after this, the Armorial Seal was incorporated into the design of Angove wine labels and has been used ever since in this manner.

The 1956 flood

8

Renmark Distillery, August 1956 – during the River Murray flood, the largest on record

Two calamities befell the Renmark Winery and Distillery during 1956 – a fire and a flood. The fire, in January 1956, destroyed a supply store and its contents. Fortunately prompt action confined the fire to a single building; it could have been much more damaging had it spread to the wine and spirit storage areas.

Following the serious flooding of the River Murray in 1917 and 1931, high water levels were experienced in 1939, 1952 and 1955, but it was not until 1956 that another major flood occurred. On 28 June the waters reached a height of 24'10" [7.57 m] at Renmark wharf and they were to rise even further, the largest flood ever experienced. Arch Grosvenor in his book, *The Murray Pioneer Flood Diary* (1957), stated that, 'It is almost impossible to establish an accurate assessment of the total loss in … this record flood.'

Many commentators remarked that the emergency brought about a wonderful cooperation and friendship among the locals and the many helpers who came to Renmark to give assistance.

The 1956 flood extended over a period of seven months. It reached serious proportions in June, peaked in August (30'7¾" [9.34 m] at the Renmark wharf) and had not fully retreated until January 1957. By August many people living in the town had been evacuated. Sandbags and earth levees surrounded Renmark and there were 20 pumps lifting water from the towns underground drainage system back into the river. Vehicle access to the town was limited. Tom Angove made the new bond store building available for storing the furniture of employees who had to evacuate their homes.

A serious breach of the levee occurred on 19 August 1956 at the RIT No 3 Pumping Station near the Angove winery. The break was through the bottom of the bank and the rush of water rapidly eroded the core of the bank. A large steel plate was lowered into the water on the outside face of the bank and a tarpaulin was secured over the plate. This restrained the flow giving the working crew time to bolster up the inner section and to build a sand-bag wall over two metres high in an arc across the corner where the breach was located.

The leak was through a section of the bank near a right-angled corner. As the sandbag wall was extended upwards, earth backing several metres wide was packed around it. All the while, the water was pouring through the decayed bank into the winery grounds. When the wall had reached the height of the water outside and the backing was all around, the channel under the bridge was plugged with sandbags and the rest then filled with earth. As soon as the channel was plugged it was a race against the rising water, which was then being held up, and the very imminent collapse of the leaking bank.

This action sealed the leak and after a further 24 hours of non-stop work, it was considered secure. At one stage, about half way to achieving the plug, a tunnel broke through to the north of the sandbag wall. This was plugged by digging down from the top of the bank to intercept the tunnel and then packing the hole with part-filled sandbags by a person standing in the hole and using his feet to place and pack the bags. As these were placed, earth was shovelled in and eventually the gallery was sealed. The man in the hole was Tom Angove.

Fifty-three years later, Tom's wife, Beverley, who was at the winery during the emergency, recounted: 'Tom went down to plug the hole in the bank, which he successfully did. When he came back up, he had virtually passed out from the cold and exhaustion. He was taken into the office and laid on a sofa. I bathed him with warm water and he came around. I think if he hadn't acted when he did he would have lost the winery.'

The determined effort by all concerned had 'saved not only one of Renmark's vital industries but also its main pumping station'.

Developments at Tea Tree Gully

Vintage at Tea Tree Gully in the 1940–1950s was around 350–400 tons of which more than half came from Angove vineyards. The balance came from long-time suppliers, mainly in the local district. In the 1940s there was considerable interest in expanding vineyard plantings in the Modbury and Golden Grove areas. Wynns, Penfolds and Douglas A. Tolley Pty Ltd acquired land in the area, as did Angove's Ltd. In May 1947 Angove purchased 62½ acres (25 ha) at Modbury, of which 50 acres (20 ha) were already planted (Pedro Ximenes and Grenache) and they planted a further 8½ acres to Shiraz.

Considerable replanting occurred at the Tea Tree Gully vineyards in the 1950s and 1960s, largely replacing varieties that were no longer in demand. The new plantings included Riesling, Semillon, Cabernet Sauvignon, Shiraz and Mataro. Palomino was also replanted for the production of base wines for sherry.

Arthur Hall retired as manager at Tea Tree Gully in August 1946. Perce Goodes continued to manage the vineyards until 1967, when his son, Ray, followed him as vineyard manager. Ray joined Angove when he was 15 as 'the boy about the place'. He started in the era of horses, which he loved, and later progressed to tractors. Working with horses was labour intensive and all vineyard practices occurred at a much slower pace than today.

'The company had up to 12 horses, Clydesdales and Percherons. We generally worked them as six pairs or individually for some operations. They were housed at The Farm. We would feed them at the end of the day and Bill [Hockey] would feed them again at 9 o'clock and would get up at 6 am to feed them before we stared the day's work.

'Spraying was done with a 60-gallon capacity sprayer with two horizontal arms that went out over the top of the vine rows. Each arm had four double spray nozzles. The height of the arms could be altered according to the size of the vines. It was drawn by a single horse. You were very exposed and after a day's spraying with bluestone everyone knew what you had been doing.'

Ray Goodes recalled, 'Vintage was the busiest time of the year. In addition to our own employees, we took on up to 17 casuals during harvest. We picked into 4-gallon kero tins and a full-time carrier was kept busy taking the full tins to the trolley. In my early years we carted the grapes in two four-wheeled trollies each with three horses, two in the poles and one in the lead. Loads were about 3 tons and it would take about 1½ hours to go from Tolley Road to the winery and back by when the second trolley would be loaded ready to go. We would do about four loads a day.

'We were still using horses when the Modbury vineyards came on. It was a long, slow haul from there up to the Gully. I always seemed to get pulled over by the Department of Transport people to be weighed. You could only carry a certain weight on a metal 2½-inch rim. If it was over-weight, I used to say to the weighbridge operator, "It's our last load." We had lots of last loads!'

In the 1940s, vines were still grown as bush vines or on a single wire trellis. 'We first used a double wire in the early 1960s, one at 18 inches and the other at 3 feet. At first the change wasn't universally accepted. Other changes that occurred; we planted vines on the contour and adopted a lot more rod pruning rather than spurs – with good results.'

Perce Goodes was acting manager at Tea Tree Gully for two years until the appointment of Roger Wyatt in September 1969. Roger's background was not in the wine industry but as a leading-hand detailer in the tool shop at General Motors Holden at Woodville. His joining Angove came about in an unusual manner. 'I was working part-time at the Findon Hotel and was interested in wine. The Dalgety's rep [representative] asked if the hotel would be interested in carrying Angove wines. That wasn't my decision to make but I did go and have a look at the winery at Tea Tree Gully. I was taken by the lovely old buildings but thought, there's not much happening here. I wrote to the company – I didn't know anyone there – and got a 'phone call from Mr Tom Angove. He invited my wife and I to visit Renmark to discuss things with him. The outcome was that he offered me a job at Tea Tree Gully.' Tom Angove appointed Roger as Branch Manager with instructions to 'put in place what I thought it could be'.

Tregrehan Vineyards, April 1974

At the time there were eight full-time employees in the cellars and about 14 in the vineyard. Ray Goodes was the vineyard manager and Max Steinwedel was cellar foreman. Roger was put in charge of the winemaking and was instructed in winemaking and laboratory procedure by Bob Hill, the winemaker at Renmark. Following vintage, the wine from Tea Tree Gully was transported to Renmark for finishing and blending, and base wines for Flor sherry production were brought from Renmark.

Wine marketing, brands and packaging

Angove's London-based company, Dominion Wines celebrated its silver jubilee in November 1954. Dominion was one of the largest importers of Australian wines to Great Britain. However, Australia had not regained the level of exports that existed before World War II because of increasing production and freight costs, and the erosion of the Empire preferential duty.

Although overall Australian wine exports had declined, Angove was holding its position in the market. In 1956–1957 it was the third largest wine shipper from Australia and in 1957–1958 ranked second to The Emu Wine Company.

The decade following the 1960s saw a decrease in exports. An increase in custom tariffs, together with eroding benefits from Empire preference arrangements and the advent of the EEC, weighed heavily against the wine export trade. Dominion Wines ceased trading in 1968.

Winemakers Robert Hill and David Whillas, 1974

Some of Angove's other export markets fared better than Great Britain. South-East Asia had been an important market for over 30 years. In the early 1960s Angove started to export table wines, such as Bookmark Riesling and Brightlands Burgundy, in addition to the traditional lines of brandy and fortified wines, to Singapore and Malaya. Other markets included various British Commonwealth nations, including Hong Kong, Jamaica, Barbados, Trinidad and Tanganyika. Most of the market was for bulk wines that the buyers then bottled under either an Angove label or their own.

Canada became a valuable market during World War II when the country was cut off from her traditional wine suppliers in Europe. Tom Angove and John Guinand negotiated a sound market for Angove's wines, notably Marko vermouths, in Canada.

Until the mid-1950s, Angove sold most of its product in bulk. The exception to this was the bottled trade for St Agnes Brandy. With increased marketing of bottled wines, the name St Agnes was withdrawn from use on its wine labels and 'Angove's' as a brand name was introduced along with wine names such as Brightlands Burgundy, Bookmark Riesling and Tregrehan Claret. Since that time, St Agnes has been reserved exclusively for brandy.

Chateau Downunda label

In October 1965 Angove registered one of their most famous export labels, Château Downunda. A dry red table wine was marketed under this and the Carpentaria label, reflecting the greatly improved standard of Australian wines being exported to Great Britain.

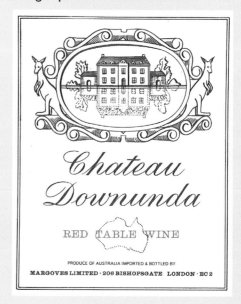

ANGOVE'S
SPECIAL
Fino Dry
AUSTRALIAN SHERRY
(PALE DRY WINE)
— CELLAR BOTTLED —
PRODUCED & BOTTLED BY
ANGOVE'S PTY. LTD.
RENMARK. SOUTH AUSTRALIA
PRODUCE OF AUSTRALIA
ALCOHOL 17.5% BY VOLUME • CONTENTS 1 PINT 9 FL OZ
IMPORTED & DISTRIBUTED BY KOPPEL INDUSTRIES, INC.
WILMINGTON • CALIFORNIA, U.S.A.

ANGOVE'S
Tregrehan
RESERVE
AUSTRALIAN CLARET
PRODUCED & BOTTLED BY
ANGOVE'S PTY. LTD.
RENMARK. SOUTH AUSTRALIA

ANGOVE'S
Tregrehan
RESERVE
CLARET
1983
A blend of Shiraz and Cabernet Sauvignon,
giving a fresh appealing dry red wine style,
balanced by subtle oak character.
CELLAR BOTTLED
PRODUCED & BOTTLED BY
ANGOVES PTY. LTD. BOOKMARK AVE. RENMARK, S.A- 5341
11.5% ALC/VOL PRODUCE OF AUSTRALIA 750 ml

'angel'
GINGER WINE
女仙
酒薑寶大
THE HEALTH DRINK
PRODUCT OF AUSTRALIA
PRODUCED & BOTTLED BY:
ANGOVE'S PTY. LTD.
ESTD. 1884
RENMARK, S.A.
IMPORTED BY:
TAN CHIANG HAK.
749 UPPER SERANGOON ROAD,
SINGAPORE 19

THE FAMILY WINE

...y years of manufacturing experience is behind the production of ..."ANGEL" Ginger Wine — a creditable testimony to its unrivalled ...lities.

...from the choicest ginger, it is
　　　Exquisite in taste
　　　Delicate in aroma
　　　Mild in action
　　　Smooth to the throat and
　　　Free from sourness

...Unique Combination of Merits is rare. "ANGEL" Ginger Wine
...y preserves intact the health-giving properties of natural ginger
...s forth those properties to their highest state of perfection,
...ng purity and mellowness, which made it, for more than two
...a favourite of the whole family.

...erent digestive ... qualities of ginger automatically suggest
..."Ginger Wine the natural "Round-up" to a hearty meal.

PRODUCT OF AUSTRALIA

SEVOGNA
HERB & IRON
Tonic wine
Recommended for its incomparable tonic and restorative properties. This
Tonic is a true restorative of specific merit and incomparable worth for
Debility, Sleeplessness, Fatigue, Anaemia and General Sickness
NET CONTENTS: 13 FLUID OUNCES
PRODUCED BY
ANGOVE'S LTD. OF RENMARK, SOUTH AUSTRALIA
IMPORTED AND DISTRIBUTED IN HONG KONG BY
H. RUTTONJEE & SON LTD.

施華...
此酒為...得之
密方法，内含...
體靈弱者，確...
之功，病後眼...更能令身體迅速復
元，其醫療價值之高，無有出其右者

SEVOGNA This Tonic, a true restorative, is of specific merit and incomparable
worth for all Debility, Sleeplessness, Fatigue, Anaemia and General Sickness.
Tonic wine. It is compounded from herbs, salts of Iron and the finest natural red
wine guaranteed for its quality and strength. The innovation and blending
is carried out in time honoured manner protecting the health restorative and therapeutic
properties of the ingredients so that the greatest possible benefit is derived from this wonderful
health-giving and restorative properties. In sickness and convalescence it is invaluable and if
taken whilst in good health it is a protective against debility and collapse.

原　用　方　法
每回三次，每次一小杯，於飯前或飯後服
用，夾眠者，臨睡前多服一次，即可見効

DIRECTIONS : A wineglassful 3 times a day before or after meals; and for relief of insomnia
a further wineglassful at bedtime. For its full protective value it can be taken at regular intervals
throughout the day and at night.

VINTAGE 1967
ANGOVE'S
Tregrehan
RESERVE
CLARET
PRODUCED & BOTTLED BY
...OVE'S PTY. LTD.
...NMARK AVENUE. RENMARK
... SOUTH AUSTRALIA
...PRODUCE OF AUSTRALIA 26 FL OZ imperial

ESTABLISHED IN THE YEAR 1884
Angove's
Brightland's
RESERVE
BURGUNDY
PRODUCED & BOTTLED BY
ANGOVE'S PTY LTD.
RENMARK. SOUTH AUSTRALIA
NET · 13 FLUID OUNCES

ESTABLISHED IN THE YEAR 1884
Angove's
Brightland's
RESERVE
BURGUNDY
PRODUCED & BOTTLED BY
ANGOVE'S PTY. LTD.
BOOKMARK AVE. RENMARK, STH. AUSTRALIA
metric 739 ml • PRODUCE OF AUSTRALIA • 26 FL OZ imperial

The one-millionth case of Stone's Green Ginger Wine produced in Australia.
(L to R): Doug Crittenden, Mrs Margaret (Peggy) Maxwell, Chairman of Stone's of London, and John Angove

Stone's Green Ginger Wine

Five decades ago, Stone's Green Ginger Wine was a little-known label in Australia. Today it is one of Angove Family Winemaker's best-known products. In 1963, Finsbury Distillery Company Ltd of London was looking for a winemaker in Australia who would produce and market Stone's (as it is generally called) under licence in Australia, the Far East and the South-West Pacific. Various large Australian wine companies had been approached but none showed much interest. Tom Angove, however, saw potential in the arrangement and an agreement was signed. The venture between the two companies soon proved a success and the brand attained a strong position in the Australasian market. In March 1980, the chairman of Stone's of London, Mrs Margaret (Peggy) Maxwell, visited Australia in order to present the one-millionth case of Stone's to be sold in Australia since its introduction 17 years earlier.

In June 1964 Finsbury Distillery amalgamated with Matthew Clark & Sons. The arrangements with Angove were not affected by this change in management.

In the 1980s the range of Stone's products was expanded with the addition of Stone's Mac (Ginger Wine and Scotch Whisky), Stone's 1912 Exhibition and Stone's Ginger Cooler, a light ginger and fruit-flavoured drink.

Stone's is named for Joseph Stone (1809–1896) who established a wholesale wine merchant business in 1848 and was appointed distributor for George Bishop & Sons' Finsbury Distillery. The distillery was established by James Bishop at Holborn, London in 1740. In 1875 when the registration of trademarks was introduced, Finsbury Distillery registered the Joseph Stone's Original Green Ginger Wine label which had white printing on a bottle-green background. The original of the present design, which includes the Arms of the City of London, together with the motto *Domine Dirige Nos* – literally 'Lord direct us' – was registered in 1886.

Development of the 'Bag-in-Box'

Tom Angove had a world first with the introduction in September 1965 of the 'bag-in-box' wine packaging, a design that has become the very familiar 'wine cask'. Angove's 'bag of wine' had taken two years to develop and when the one-gallon pack was introduced it was regarded by the media as an 'extremely novel idea'. The 'bag-in-box' was developed by Tom Angove and Letters Patent No. 280826 was issued to the Company on 20 April 1965. The invention was officially registered as 'an improved container and pack for liquids'. The design was similar to the present day wine cask or soft pack, that is, it comprised a plastic bag that collapsed as the wine was withdrawn, such that air did not come into contact with the wine.

The initial releases were one-gallon packs of red wine, white wine, port, sweet sherry and Muscat. The container was not intended to replace glass bottles but was for consumers who liked to buy wine in bulk, as they had done when stone jars were in common use. Wytt Morrô & Son of Adelaide did the graphic design of the packaging.

The concept was sound but the 'bag-in-box' suffered a number of technical problems. Poor shelf-life caused by the permeability of the plastic bag and resealing the bag could not be easily overcome. The pack proved that it had great market potential but because of technical problems, Angove withdrew from the market in 1971. In subsequent years they watched as fellow winemakers followed the packaging lead they had set, only to experience similar difficulties with the pack. Eventually, the design was improved (including the introduction of a tap and research into more suitable plastics by CSIRO scientist Dr Eric Davis) and by 1990 around 65% of all table wine sold in Australia was in a wine cask (AWBC Annual Report). Angove's re-entered the cask market (as it was now generally known) in 1984 with their Paddle Wheel 5 litre range of wines. The range continued until 2009 when the company again withdrew from the soft pack market.

The Angove wine cask was officially recognised as a BankSA Heritage Icon in 2006.

United Kingdom, are marketing these packs in London.

The ease of pouring from the snipped-off opening in the neck of the plastic bag (ensconced in the cardboard box) is demonstrated by Mr. Bill Marshall, Works Manager of Angove's Pty. Ltd., protographed with a specimen of the new "Bag of Wine."

Angove's Works Manager and Company Director, Bill Marshall, demonstrating Angove's pioneering Bag in a Box, September 1965

Nanya Vineyard

Until the 1960s most of the grapes processed at the Renmark winery were purchased from Riverland growers. In January 1962 Tom Angove finalised the purchase of 2000 acres (809 ha) of land at Murtho, east of Renmark, and fronting the River Murray. The object of the purchase was to develop the company's own vineyards. Angove still intended taking grapes from their traditional grower suppliers, in fact, they would remain their principal source of grapes. The purpose of the Nanya development was to supply the winery with the newly introduced grape varieties that were in demand for table wines, and to take up the shortfall from the eventual loss of their vineyards at Tea Tree Gully in the face of urban expansion.

Tom Angove carrying a case of St Agnes Brandy to be sent to Mannum on the final journey of P.S. Marion, June 1963 – the Brandy was destined for the cellars at Buckingham Palace where it duly arrived in August 1963

The vineyard's name is taken from Nanya, the 'head-man' of the Danggali Aboriginal people who occupied the country to the north of Renmark when European settlers first came to the Riverland area.

The vineyard project was planned by Tom Angove and carried out by W.C. (Bill) Crowe. Planting began in 1969 and the irrigation system was progressively extended over the next few years to cover an area of 480 ha. Much of the original planting material came from Tea Tree Gully, from Angove's own vineyards and Wynn's Wynvale Vineyards. The varieties planted in 1969–1970 were Cabernet Sauvignon, Riesling, Shiraz, Trebbiano (also known as Ugni Blanc or White Hermitage), Grenache, Sauvignon Blanc, Doradillo, Mataro and Malbec. The cuttings were ground cured and planted out direct in the vineyard rows with a take-rate of 85–95%.

A nursery operation was set up to propagate planting material of new grape varieties that were being released by the South Australian Department of Agriculture for commercial development. The newer varieties included Gewürztraminer, Pinot Noir, Chardonnay, Carignan, Colombard, Sauvignon Blanc, Gamay Beaujolais, Chenin Blanc, Sylvaner, Malbec, Rubired, Ruby Cabernet, Chardonnay, Merlot and Tarango. The suitability of some of the varieties for the region was largely unknown; this was an experimental period for the new vineyard.

Nanya Vineyards – the statistics for this huge vineyard are impressive. By 1985 the vineyard covered 480 ha (1186 acres) and contained 263,070 trellis posts, 14,688 strainer posts, 1516 km of high-tensile steel trellis wire, and 197 tonnes of steel for trellis heads suitable for mechanical harvesting. The planting totalled 810,540 vines.

By 1972, 342,000 vines had been established and the first crop harvested. The scale of the vineyard meant that hand-picking was not going to be practical. The first mechanical harvester was used in 1973 and additional machines were subsequently purchased.

Developments at Renmark

Tom Angove oversaw considerable expansions at the Renmark Winery and Distillery in the 1970s. Land adjacent to the winery was purchased, floodbanks were upgraded and landscaping was undertaken. The under-roof floor space was increased by over 48,000 square feet (4600 square metres), storage tank and wine maturation capacity was increased by nearly 2 million litres and brandy maturation capacity by 500,000 litres. Refrigeration and cooling capacity were increased with the addition of another 30 tonne, three bank, ultra-cooler and two evaporation units of 50 tonnes each. Ever looking to try new things, Tom became interested in using stainless steel for the construction of fermenting and storage tanks.

Return to flying – At much the same time as Nanya was 'getting off the ground' Tom Angove did a refresher flying course. Tom learnt to fly during World War II and flew rescue missions from north Queensland. When he stepped out of a Sikorski 0S2U5 for the last time in 1944 he vowed never to fly again. However, the demands of a company based at Renmark and the need for regular trips to Adelaide re-awakened his interest in flying. In December 1965 the Company purchased a Beechcraft Musketeer, the first in a series of Beechcraft aircrafts. A Beech Debonair and then a twin-engine Beech Baron soon followed. Four years later, Tom's son John trained for his Private Pilot's licence. Both Tom and John achieved a standard to obtain Command instrument ratings.

Tom continued the Angove family tradition of industry involvement. In October 1971, he was elected chairman of the Council of the Australian Wine Research Institute, for a three-year term. The AWRI was established in 1955 to undertake and coordinate research on wine in Australia. Tom had been a member of the Council and a deputy member for a number of years prior to becoming its chairman. He served two terms as chairman in the period 1971 to 1977. He was also a member of the Executive of the Australian Wine and Brandy Producers' Association, serving from 1973 to 1987. He was Chair of the Brandy Sub-committee 1986–1987 and Chair of the Technical Sub-committee 1979 to 1982. He was also a Council member of the Wine Committee of The Royal Agricultural and Horticultural Society of South Australia for 41 years. In 1977 he was awarded the Queen Elizabeth II Silver Medal for services to the wine industry.

John Angove joined the family business in January 1972 and, along with Bob Abbott, was appointed a director of Angove's Pty Ltd. After completing his secondary education at St Peter's College, Adelaide, John took a Bachelor of Science degree at the University of Adelaide, and followed this with a Business Studies course at the South Australian Institute of Technology. In June 1970 he travelled overseas, visiting South-East Asia, Great Britain, Europe and North America, spending 18 months visiting the wine areas of France, Italy and Germany. He worked for a time at the Australian Wine Centre in London and gained a valuable insight into the issues facing Australian wines in the British market. It was very apparent that English consumers still did not accept Australian wine as wine of quality. This was seen as an opportunity for the company.

Aerial view of Angove's Renmark Distillery, c. 1968

12

Loss of the Tea Tree Gully vineyards

Significant changes were also about to occur at Tea Tree Gully. Some were changes the company could not have predicted and were beyond the company's control.

In the period 1960 to 1975 the vintage at Tea Tree Gully ranged from 160 and 469 tonnes, depending on seasonal conditions. Most of the grapes came from Angove vineyards but the company continued to purchase grapes from local growers, many of whom had been suppliers for decades. A new office, laboratory, cellar door sales area and warehouse were built in 1972.

John Angove with Bill Hockey, Angove Family Winemakers longest-serving employee at St Agnes Cellars. Bill retired in January 1973 after being with the company for 61 years. He had been in charge of the Tregrehan and The College vineyards for over three decades.

Scenes from the penultimate vintage at Tea Tree Gully, February 1981 –

Clockwise from top left: Roger Wyatt in the vintage cellar

Section of the Riesling vineyard

Flor sherry storage, Tea Tree Gully, 1974

Arn Bowden unloading grapes in to the crusher

Top right: Roger Wyatt and Ray Goodes, 2010
Centre: section of Angove's Scrub, now Angove Conservation Park, and part of the 1904 cellar building
Bottom right: cellar door sales at Tea Tree Gully

Load of wooden storage tanks ready for transfer to Renmark from Tea Tree Gully, 1977

The unpredicted event occurred on 17 October 1974. That day the South Australian Land Commission compulsorily acquired the Angove vineyards on Tolley Road and at Modbury. The role of the SALC was to identify and acquire land for future urban expansion. In the Modbury – Tea Tree Gully district, a total of 390 ha were acquired: Mount Adam Estate Pty Ltd 160 ha, Douglas A. Tolley Pty Ltd 49 ha, Penfold Wines Pty Ltd 65 ha, St Peter's College (known as 'The College Block' or 'Lokans') 30 ha, and Angove 90 ha.

It was a sad day both for the company and the vineyard workers. Ray Goodes recalls Tom Angove coming to break the news to the men. 'Mr Angove came from Renmark to see us. He arrived at the winery and walked around the creek, kicking stones up as he went. This was unusual for him as he generally came straight out with anything he had to say to us. When he did speak he just said, 'Ray, we're finished down here, the Government wants the land for housing.'

The company contested the acquisition by all means possible, but to no avail. The acquisition meant that they had lost a significant source of high quality fruit. Their top table wines were blends of wines from the Adelaide and River Murray regions and the base wines for the Fino Flor Dry Sherry was Pedro Ximenes from Tea Tree Gully. The company had expected that urban encroachment would eventually force them out of Tea Tree Gully, but not as early as 1974. A replanting program was well advanced and as recently as August 1974, 1.8 ha of Tregrehan Vineyards was replanted to Riesling vines.

The last full vintage at St Agnes was in 1975 when 414 tonnes were processed. The 1982 vintage marked the end of an era at Tea Tree Gully. This was the 90th vintage at St Agnes and the last. Some 15½ tonnes of Riesling were processed for Flor sherry base. The vines were removed in June 1982 and the land was later sold for residential subdivision. The Angove's Scrub portion of the property was purchased by the State Government in 1985 and is now Angove Conservation Park. Tom Angove and his cousin, Dr Roger Angove, installed a seat in the park in memory of their grandfather, Dr W.T. Angove, recognising his involvement with wildlife preservation, long before it was in the general public consciousness.

Restored St Agnes Cellar buildings, 1982

13

A changing marketplace

In 1974 Angove released the first of their varietal table wine range. The first wines under the *Angove's Varietal* label were experimental releases Rhine Riesling, Sauvignon Blanc, Chenin Blanc and Sylvaner from the 1974 vintage; other varietals followed in subsequent years – Sylvaner, Chenin Blanc, Chardonnay, Traminer, French Colombard, Shiraz, Pinot Noir and Cabernet Sauvignon. The new range of wines was soon winning awards at wine shows. The outstanding 1981 Rhine Riesling was awarded the Qantas/ Wine Society Trophy, as well as two Gold Medals, at the 1981 Melbourne Wine Show.

During 1979 changes in the market place made it evident that the company needed to take greater control of the marketing of its own products. The agency arrangements that had been the sole means of distribution were not meeting the needs of a rapidly changing market. The first branch office to be established was in Sydney in 1979 and branches in Melbourne, Brisbane and Perth followed. The New South Wales branch was managed by K.W.H. (Ken) Stevens. Ken came to Angove in 1964 from Caldbeck MacGregor & Company in Singapore, the agents for Angove wines in South East Asia. He remained with Angove until he retired in 1994 and then served as a Board member of Angove's Pty Ltd until 2003.

At the same time as the state branches were established, a new wholesale distribution centre for South Australia was built at St Agnes. The altered system gave the company direct control over its sales and marketing and quickly showed the advantages that such

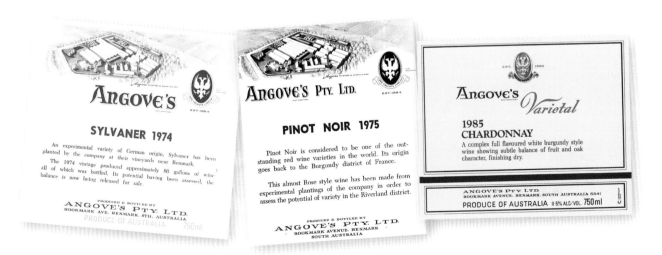

control provides. An ever-increasing percentage of the company's output was being marketed under the Angove label with a resultant decrease in reliance on the 'bulk wine' trade.

James Kelly managed the Melbourne branch for 28 years from July 1980. Jim joined Angove in September 1976 after having worked in the wool industry and then in wine and spirit retailing in the UK.

As Jim recalled, 'On 28 July 1985 John Angove signed the company's first agency agreement with Junji Nakamura, Managing Director in Australia for Suntory, for the distribution of their spirits and liqueurs but principally Midori liqueur. This brand grew from 200 cases a year in 1985 to over 20,000 by 1993, but more importantly, the Japanese style of budgeting, marketing and sales proved invaluable in the growth and development of the Victorian Branch. We wanted to be the best in the Company for sales of cartons, gross dollars and net profit, a feat we achieved repeatedly.'

A potentially major setback occurred in December 1985 when the Melbourne branch was destroyed by fire. Jim recalled, 'The event showed the character and the resourcefulness of the Company. Within two days we had orders flowing to Renmark and stock being despatched to retailers in Melbourne over night, with the Renmark staff working extra time to keep us going. At the Melbourne end we set up an office in a staff member's home and within two weeks had temporary premises set up nearby. It was six months before we moved back to our Geddes Street premises.'

Major changes occurred in the company when Bob Abbott retired as company secretary on 21 December 1979 after 35 years with the company, and Bill Crowe, the 'Father of Nanya Vineyard', retired in November 1985 after 17 years as vineyard manager.

Although retired, Bob Abbott continued to be responsible for Tom Angove family's financial matters until he did finally retire in 2006. He returned on a number of occasions as acting-secretary. Being of the old school he was initially sceptical as to how he would

cope with the new computer systems, but as in the past, he was undaunted by the job and adapted his thinking as required. As John Angove commented, 'His contribution and dedication to the family company over many decades ranks with the highest.' In retirement Bob moved to Port Lincoln to be closer to his family. He died in September 2009.

Collingwood Sponsorship

Jim Kelly recalled: Sponsorships of key organisations became a part of our activities to drive the name Angove in our market place. The return of 500cc Motor Sport to Phillip Island in 1989 and our national involvement in the Spastic Society's Miss Australia Quest had long lasting effects. Our other highlight was the flow on from the 1990 AFL Grand Final where we were sponsors of Collingwood Football Club from 1988 to 1995. In conjunction with their marketing department we arranged to produce a Premiership Port should they win the Premiership.

Collingwood wanted a labelled bottle of port on each of the tables at the Premiership Dinner, so after being given the labels on the morning of the game, 5 October 1990, I took them back to our warehouse where we had the staff set to start labelling should Collingwood win, less one label and bottle which we took into the MCG to open after the final siren. The game was won; I took sufficient labelled product into the dinner venue the Southern Cross Hotel for the evening and had enough stock to cover the souvenir department at the club.

However, on Sunday sales took off and we quickly ran out of stock. The next day, Monday 7 October, was a public holiday in South Australia. I telephoned Renmark and Mr T.W. [Angove] answered the 'phone. I detailed what has occurred in Melbourne, and he replied that he was amazed that we had any stock at all left. I asked him to break the rules in his supply book and for 10 pallets of port to be in Melbourne by Wednesday. Early the next day I telephoned the bottling hall to see when the port was scheduled to be bottled, to be told that it was 'going down the line now; we were all 'phoned at home yesterday'.

That was the first of many pallets for Collingwood. Our sponsorship arrangement with Collingwood was to pay them a royalty per bottle. The first cheque given at the end of October was $50,000 and by December a further $30,000, with others following to give a total exceeding $100,000. As a marketing exercise, the product was pitched at under $10 to be affordable for all supporters. The bottles today are collector's items.

Fine wine production

With the expansion of the Angove vineyards and the growing supply of premium grape varieties, marketing strategies were directed increasingly towards the wine market. While this market was developing, brandy sales were in decline. John Angove recalled the period as 'years of chaos and despair from a brandy producer's point of view. In the early 1970s, Australian brandy in Australia was the spirit of choice. We then went through those amazing duty increases by the Commonwealth Government, commencing in 1972. Without a doubt, the other spirits weathered that battering very much better than brandy. Since the 1970s the brandy sales graph has been constantly downwards, with occasional periods of levelling off, but then it seems to sink down again … it's still hardly a buoyant market.'

However, under these difficult circumstances St Agnes brandy has continued to prosper and grow. Twenty years ago it had 8–9% of the Australian brandy market, and today it is more like 40%. A number of other producers have left the market during these years but perhaps, as John Angove observed, 'it's a case of the continuing high quality of the product that allows it to flourish'.

Roseworthy Agricultural College oenology graduate Michael Farmilo was vintage winemaker and quality controller from 1977 to 1984. It was during Michael's time with the company that their range of premium table wines began winning critical acclaim, a trend that has continued to the present time. In 1985 Frank Newman was appointed as chief winemaker. Another Roseworthy graduate, Frank continued the high standard set by his predecessor in the field of table wine production.

Frank joined Angove at much the same time as Andrew Darby who was to become the company's Operations Manager. Andrew recalled Frank as 'a really good winemaker'. At that time, the winemaking facilities were geared to the production of fortified wines and brandy, rather than quality table wines, but. 'Frank made some really good wines under these conditions.' During Frank's time with Angove, the company 'went from being known as distillers to being noted as winemakers. John [Angove] wanted Angove to be known as winemakers and not just for brandy, fortified wines and green ginger wine.'

At the time, Angove was not in the position financially to undertake significant upgrades in winemaking facilities. As Andrew Darby saw it, 'Tom [Angove] had a mechanical bent and the desire to keep old machinery operating as efficiently as possible was important to him. Besides, he liked tinkering with machinery. It made for interesting times and certainly tested our mechanical skills.' He recalled that they worked with what they had, but machinery breakdowns meant that his early vintages were often 60- to 70-hour weeks. The 1986 vintage saw the installation of new refrigeration equipment, rotary vacuum filtration, an additional 850,000 litres of insulated storage capacity, improved skins and seeds handling facility, and improved inert gas protection for table wines.

'Refrigeration is a necessary evil for wineries. It is costly to install and operate but is essential. In the mid 1980s, Angove had three separate refrigeration units that were not really adequate for the size of their fermentation. One of the company's fitters, Ken Brakewell, had great skills with refrigeration. Ken got the workshop to combine the three pieces of equipment so the winemakers would have greater cooling facility. It was an ingenious bit of engineering. He had us build a system that could be added to over time as funds permitted.

'Ideally, you plan your needs according to known climatic extremes. I recall one vintage we had seven days in succession of over 40 °C, peaking at 47 °C. This really tested the winemakers, and the engineers!'

Andrew Darby came to Angove with a background as a fitter and machinist and had worked previously in this capacity at Berri Estate Wines. He began as a fitter on the bottling line and was soon made Workshop Foreman. 'We did everything here ourselves, from rebuilding water pumps to building storage tanks. At that time, we saw Tom [Angove] every day. He had a great interest in engineering, probably as great as his interest in winemaking. I recall an occasion in about 1989 when Tom was in the pumping pit at Nanya in his tweed suit with spanner in hand working with me on one of the pumps. That's the sort of man he was. We struck up a good working relationship pretty early on. He was a big influence on me and fostered my interest in engineering.

'That's not to say we didn't put each other in our place at times. One time I was fabricating a capping race. I sensed that there was someone behind me and switched off the welder. There was Tom and he said, "You know that's not going to work?" I responded, and probably with a few poorly chosen words, saying, "If you don't leave me alone, we'll never find out!"

'We had a good relationship for many years to follow. He had a method of telling you that you might not be looking at something in the right light. I was young and fairly determined at the time and I probably didn't see the advice coming but it was there.

'The Maintenance Foreman's job was pretty easy because the guys around me were so good. Neale Dunhill is an exceptional fabricator and Dave Wilson was a good all rounder, for instance. Between us, we could pretty well build anything, and we did.'

The coming of change

By the mid 1980s the role of the next generation was coming to the fore. Tom Angove retired as managing director in January 1983 and was succeeded by John. Tom remained as Chairman of Directors, retiring in 2001. In December 1993, the Winemakers' Federation of Australia invested Tom as a Patron in recognition of his

Tom Angove in the brandy store, 1997. Photo courtesy The Advertiser

outstanding contribution to the industry. The following month, he was appointed a Member in the General Division of the Order of Australia in the 1994 Australia Day Honours List. Tom's 35-year term as managing director saw enormous growth in the company's operations, making the company one of the largest family-owned wineries in Australia. His exacting nature and high standard of operations gave the company an enviable reputation for quality, stability and integrity, the very characteristics that epitomised Tom Angove.

Until the mid-1980s, the company was still very much a producer of brandy and fortified wines. A large proportion of the Australian wine industry was still in its infancy where the production of table wines were concerned. Angove's best-known brands were St Agnes Brandy, Marko Vermouth and Stone's Green Ginger Wine. A huge change in emphasis and direction has occurred since the 1980s with the company positioning itself as premium winemakers, under the banner Angove Family Winemakers.

Twenty years ago, the company was producing small quantities of fine wine but, as John Angove recalled, 'Our whole production environment, and our method of handling fruit, was geared to produce either fortifying spirit or brandy out of every tonne of fruit that came in, and so our extraction processes for wine were not that efficient. We didn't worry if 20% of every tonne of fruit went off to spirit or brandy.

'As time went by, it became more critical that out of every tonne of fruit, we needed as much fine wine as we could produce. We didn't really want to see around a fifth used to produce spirit or brandy.'

This realisation brought about a reappraisal of the company's winemaking practices. The company had to be in the position where every tonne of fruit provided around 750 litres of wine. This became even more significant as sales of brandy and fortified wines continued to decline. As John Angove observed, 'It took an enormous amount of time, input, energy and finance to revamp the way we process grapes. I guess that has been one of the greatest changes since the 1990s that we have gone through, driven by an incredible surge of wine exports. There has also been a strong increase in sales of wine in the domestic market. Today we produce brandy but almost no fortifying spirit and simply purchase our spirit requirements.

'This change has released a large tonnage of fruit that now goes into fine wines. So really without a significant increase in total volume throughput, we have been able to increase our wine volumes by an enormous amount.'

The change in approach has enabled the company to ensure a greater continuity of quality. 'Previously we were able to make relatively small parcels of high quality wine. The current winemaking system has enabled us to make larger volumes of quality wine, and thereby achieve a far greater penetration of quality product into the market-place. It has been a very positive change for the company.'

Nanya Vineyard redeveloped

By the early 1990s, Angove was looking to redevelop the 480-hectare Nanya Vineyard. The vines were getting old and some varieties were no longer required in the quantities that were being produced. Furthermore, the vines were on low 3 ft wide T-trellises and were difficult to harvest and prune. However, as John Angove observed, 'While there was never any doubt as to the reasons for the re-development from a viticultural point of view, it did take some time to determine if financially it was an appropriate move given the prevailing market conditions. After all, it's not a cheap exercise.

'At the time grapes were too valuable to remove – they were worth $800–$900 per tonne. We bided our time until the value started to fall. It coincided with Nick Bakkum joining the company in 2001.'

Nick Bakkum joined Angove in June 2001 to supervise the redevelopment of the vineyard. Nick came with considerable experience in vineyard development both in South Australia and interstate. Although the vineyard had been set up for mechanical harvesting, the trellising was not suited to the design of newer harvesters. Nick commented, 'I soon realised that we were tough on what we expected from our growers but we needed to be tougher on ourselves. The redevelopment was a big change in how we operate our vineyards.

'The redevelopment has focused on achieving more effective and environmentally sustainable vineyard management, and improved grape quality by controlled water application and the selection of the most appropriate vine clones and rootstocks. In the first few years of the program, the company replanted 40 hectares per year, and worked in a systematic fashion from the front of the property. At the end of harvest the next area to be replanted would be removed, the site deep ripped, the new rows surveyed, trellised and planted in August. It became an annual routine and was a part of our vineyard operations.'

The rows were turned through 90 degrees and now run east to west; they are longer and easier to work mechanically. Individual rows are 5 km [3.2 miles] long. Greater attention has been given than in the past to using the most appropriate rootstocks for site and soil conditions and then targeting the clone of the variety to the end use of the grapes. As Nick related, 'It's a natural evolution in our viticulture. We originally had around 23 varieties and there are only 3 or 4 we will not replant. Tom Angove's original choices have stood the test of time. Varieties like Palomino, Ruby Cabernet, Sylvaner and Chenin Blanc are no longer in demand and some other varieties were mainly for brandy production and we don't need thousands of tonnes of these anymore.'

Images at Nanya Vineyard –

Centre: Nick Bakkum, Vineyard Manager

Bottom left: River Murray at Whirlpool Corner, location of Angove's pumphouse

Nick commented regarding varieties grown: 'Our main plantings are of Shiraz, Chardonnay, Cabernet Sauvignon, Merlot and Sauvignon Blanc. We still grow a reasonable amount of Colombard – it does well here and is a very good blending variety. We have a very good clone of Riesling. It came from the original Tea Tree Gully vineyards. We've planted some Pinot Gris but at present have no plans to plant some of the other newer varieties, especially when we have good contract growers. We also have 30 ha of vines, mainly Shiraz and Cabernet, at our Anchorage Vineyard.'

Managing water

The irrigation system at Nanya Vineyard has been changed from overhead to computerised drip and incorporates fertigation and soil moisture monitoring systems with remote monitoring access. When Nanya was first established the overhead sprinkler system was 'state-of-the-art' technology and was far more efficient than furrow irrigation which was then still standard practice in the Riverland. The introduction of drip irrigation has resulted in a huge reduction in water use. It has also enabled increased efficiency of irrigation management and has the added advantage that fertilizers are now delivered through the system.

The restrictions on the use of irrigation water from 2007 to 2011 made vineyard operations difficult. Angove Family Winemakers found the restrictions easier to cope with because of the changes to their irrigation practices. As Nick Bakkum observed, 'We've learnt a lot because of the water restrictions. They have made us focus on something that perhaps previously we didn't need to pay much attention to. Now, if in doubt, we don't water. We've reduced the amount of water we apply and we've found that some varieties cope well with a lot less water and produce better quality fruit. The use of drip irrigation and RDI [restricted deficit irrigation] techniques have saved us a large amount of water.

'We use soil moisture probes – enviroscans – they're a very good guide but we still go out and dig holes in the ground. We used to do a lot of canopy trimming during the growing season but we've found that by managing water application this is not needed. We have seen improved canopy health and fruit quality.

'Different parts of the vineyard are targeted for different product and are managed accordingly. There is a strong emphasis on canopy management, nutrient and moisture control to set crop levels and fruit quality.'

The replanting program was put on hold in 2009 pending the lifting of water restrictions. Nick said, 'It's important to secure what you've already planted. A significant area of vineyard – 120 ha – was removed following the 2009 vintage and we later removed a further 25 ha, a block of Chardonnay. These areas were destined for replanting within five years and the company was purchasing water to irrigate them. With fruit readily available from contract growers it was decided to remove the vines. It has left a big gap in the vineyard but we will replant as and when the water or grape supply situation changes.'

A new pipeline was installed in 2008 from the River Murray to the vineyard. The original one was failing and was located in such a manner that it (and the power supply) was hard to access in an emergency. As John Angove observed, 'An enormous amount of work went into securing water delivery. With drip irrigation we needed to check it daily, especially in young vines, whereas with sprinklers, we gave it a good watering that would last 2–3 weeks. Now we can't afford the pumps to be out of action for any length of time. The old fibro pipes were a buried liability. We have renewed all the suction lines and the delivery lines from the river to the edge of Murtho Road. With drip we don't need the same pressure. It's now a reasonably secure system.'

New vineyard machinery has also been important in improving efficiencies and quality. Angove now use multi-row machinery that can spray three rows at a pass. Nick commented, 'We can do the whole property in 48 hours whereas it used to take weeks. Pruning is now done in a single pass and is precise for desired crop level.'

'Since 2000 the company has invested in a huge upgrade in machinery and vineyard technology. We're now at the forefront of viticulture after having lagged behind for some years. It's very invigorating for our staff to have this facility to be able to produce really good fruit. We always knew it could be done and now we're achieving it.'

Organic production

Another exciting change has been the company's move to organic production. As Nick Bakkum said, 'We get very little summer rain, so diseases are normally not a big issue for us. This and the fact that we had been using some organic sprays, were the major reasons to convert part of Nanya to organic production. It has been a natural progression from the work we have done in reviewing our "conventional" viticultural practices.'

Winemaker Tony Ingle sees organic production as another step in Angove wines reflecting the natural characteristics of the vineyard soils and the region's climate. 'Across the board, we are achieving enhanced flavours. Lovely wines like the Nine Vines Rosé demonstrate our philosophy of wines fitting the region. We are currently working with Tempranillo and Carignan which suit this region very well.'

A 40 hectare section of the vineyard, on northern side of Murtho Road, began conversion to organic production in 2008. It is planted to Cabernet Sauvignon, Shiraz, Merlot, Semillon and Petit Verdot. Angove Family Winemakers have been enthusiastically encouraged by David Bruer of Temple Bruer Vineyards at Langhorne Creek, often referred to as *Mr Organic of Australian Viticulture*. As John Angove said, 'David's very passionate about organic production. Our organic wines, Chardonnay and Shiraz/Cabernet, are both flavoursome wines. I recall David Bruer saying a long time ago that you will make better wine if you follow organic rules. Our organic Chardonnay is a delightful wine and in May 2009, the red wine was recognised as the *best organic wine in Australia*. The option exists to gradually extend organic production to the rest of the vineyard. It has been an exciting project.'

Angove Family Winemakers purchase fruit from contract growers and many of their Riverland growers have been supplying grapes for decades. Long-term relationships are very important. As Nick Bakkum related, 'Some of the growers have been with us for 30 to 40 years – they're very important to us and we need to work closely with them. We have appreciated their support over the years, especially as there have been times when they could have got a few more dollars elsewhere but stayed with us. Many growers are quite happy to operate on the basis of a handshake arrangement with us. We provide grower liaison and give viticultural and technical support to our growers.'

One of the most basic, but highly significant, changes that has occurred in recent years has been the breaking down of the barriers that have traditionally existed between the vineyard operations and the winemaking side of the business. This strict division of responsibility was far from peculiar to Angove Family Winemakers; it was commonplace throughout the wine industry. Growing the grapes was one thing and making the wine was quite another. Commonly there was a lack of cohesion between what fruit was being grown and what a winery needed.

Various factors have contributed to the change that has occurred at Angove Family Winemakers but some well-placed management training has been of critical importance. The dual goals have become to grow the best possible grapes for the end purpose and to produce fine wines for the market. The change has been such that the vineyard people now discuss with the winemakers, in the vineyard, what they require for the coming vintage, and they all see the wines that have been produced. The vineyard manager and the chief winemaker together visit their contract growers. As Angove Family Winemakers director Bruce McDougall observed, 'They respect each other. The company has given its people the ability to show what they can do and they're stimulated to do it. The continual improvement since 2001 has been quite remarkable.'

40 ha of Nanya Vineyard has been converted to organic production. The organic range of wines has been outstanding and in May 2008 the Shiraz Cabernet was named the best organic wine in Australia.

16

St Agnes Brandy celebrated

Australia's best-known brandy celebrated its 75th anniversary in 2000. The anniversary of the introduction of St Agnes Brandy to the marketplace was appropriately marked with an event in the cellars at Tea Tree Gully.

Angove Family Winemakers' Distillery Manager, John Norman, has worked in the distillery since 1972. He is the son of a Renmark brick-maker and having left his job with a local dairy company, went to Angove to see if any work was available. John recalled, 'I 'phoned the company and went for an interview with Mr Bob Abbott. That was on the Thursday, I started work the following Monday. I had my boiler operator's ticket – a position came up in the boiler room and after a couple of weeks I went up to the stills.' He spent a couple of weeks working with the distiller and then 'was put in the deep end'. Since then he has become a master distiller and brandy blender.

The stills remain much the same as when John started with the company. One significant change has been that the continuous still has gradually been changed over to being a stainless steel still.

Angove traditionally used Sultana and Doradillo grapes for brandy production.

Distillery Manager,
John Norman

As John said, 'These are neutral varieties. Some of the newer varieties we later used threw a haze in the brandy, due to oils separating out, so we would have to cold stabilise the brandy before bottling it.'

The company's brandy production is based around the pot still batch process followed by many years maturing in small oak casks. Four brandies are marketed under the St Agnes label – St Agnes 3-Star Brandy (2–4 years of age), St Agnes VSOP 5 Year Old Brandy (minimum age 5 years), St Agnes 30 Year Old Show Brandy and St Agnes XO Very Old Brandy which has a minimum age of 20 years, with portions of the blend 50 years of age; it is 'a super premium product that offers complexity, finesse and elegance and is the pinnacle of Australian aged spirits.'

The St Agnes 30 Year Old Show Brandy, a limited special release, was to commemorate the 75th anniversary of St Agnes Brandy. The XO Brandy is marketed in very stylish packaging and commands a premium price. As John Angove observed, 'The product is second to none – it is a very good old brandy.'

The St Agnes brandy label has evolved over time but retains the basic elements of the original design. Collotype Labels Pty Ltd of Adelaide has printed the labels since 1934. The two companies first began working together in that year when Carl Angove approached Collotype's managing director, Roy Gilbert Teakle, to create the artwork and print labels for St Agnes Brandy. The Teakle family were known as fine art and colour printers but printing wine labels was somewhat of a departure from their usual printing work. Now, over 75 years later, the relationship between the two companies remains a mutually beneficial working arrangement.

St Agnes is Australia's most highly awarded brandy, having received 18 trophies, including 'World's Best', over 70 Gold Medals and over 200 Silver and Bronze Medals in the past 30 years at Australian and international shows. St Agnes XO Brandy was awarded the 'Best in the Show' award at the 2008 and 2009 International Wine and Spirit Challenge in London. It was awarded a Gold Medal and Trophy at the 2010 Royal Adelaide Wine Show. It is indeed an iconic product of the Australian wine industry.

The St Agnes range was extended in 2006 with the introduction of grape vodka. St Agnes Silver Vodka is distilled using traditional methods and has a twist of citrus added for a smooth, subtle flavour.

The stillhouse and wood storage of brandy

Winemaking team 2006 –
Rear (L to R): Sean Schwager,
Ben Horley. Front (L to R):
Tony Ingle, Warwick Billings,
Shane Clohesy

Winemaking and winemakers

17

Frank Newman was Senior Winemaker from 1985 until 2002, variously assisted by Ian Marchant and Jane Gilham. Jane was the winemaking link between Frank and Warwick Billings who joined Angove on a contract for the 2002 vintage and later became their Senior Winemaker.

Warwick was born in Australian but spent his early decades in England where he became a cider-maker. He decided to come to Australia to obtain knowledge from the Australian wine industry and, as he said, 'take it back and make better cider. However, I got seduced by the weather and stayed.' He studied Oenology at Roseworthy and then over the next few years he worked as a winemaker at various places, one being Miranda Winery in King Valley. He recalls, 'It was through Miranda Wines that I met Jane Gilham. She was a winemaker at Angove and was looking for a winemaker – and I was looking for a job. I made contact and went for an interview with John Angove and started soon afterwards – it was a six-month vintage contract for vintage 2002.

'I started in December or January and I had another job overseas after vintage. It went pretty well and 6–8 weeks before I was to leave for overseas, Jane said she was leaving. "You can't, you're the boss!" I said. She'd been there three years as Senior Winemaker and felt it was time to move on. The HR [human resources] person, Jo McConaghy, said they wanted to talk to me about Jane's job. I'd just taken a contract in France. I asked if I could think about it while I was away. I came back.'

The 2002 vintage had given Warwick a feel for how the winemaking processes could be improved. Warwick recalled, 'I had an in-depth talk with John Angove about how I thought winemaking needed to evolve. John was extremely supportive; people probably don't appreciate the changes that occurred at that point but without him saying, "Yes, let's try that", I couldn't have done it.

'We looked to change how things were done. The company had always been pretty lean. We needed to restructure to give more winemaking ability and support. John embraced that and we put those people in place. Jane had been it plus Ben Horley and another relatively inexperienced winemaker when I got there. So, for the scale of what the company did, it was reasonably lean. By being lean it meant that the winemaking focus could get lost sometimes. My proposition was that if the company wanted to be a serious winemaker there needed to be more focus on the wines. Historically, perhaps, the focus had been more on the brandy side of things.'

The change that Warwick had in mind was perhaps not revolutionary but it was an important, basic consideration. 'The focus became that we want to do winemaking well and we set out to do that. The vineyard manager, Nick Bakkum, started just before me and he raised the professionalism and modern thinking out there in the vineyard. Winemakers aren't honest if they don't say it's down to the grapes. Nick came from a pretty industrial background at McGuigans so we had to switch his focus back to a family winemaking company. We got along well – he saw we were all going to the same place. It was not a case of them against us, which happens in a lot of companies. If he needed to talk to a winemaker at 3 o'clock in the morning, he was welcome to do so. He understood our commitment.

Alex Russell (Winemaker), Barry Goody (Cellar Hand), David Alpen (Cellar Hand), Stewart Celani (IT Support Assistant), Robert May (Cellar Hand)

'Winemaking has a lot of ownership. If I spend three months of the year not sleeping because I want the wines to be right, everyone else needs to be participating. We put together a good team. We got Tony Ingle from Hardys, Sean Schwager, a young winemaker just out of university, and Shane Clohesy, from Taltarni Wines, in a winemaking support role to do the things that slow the winemaker down, so they could focus on the winemaking.

'It's easy for winemakers to get bogged down in administration and to take on lots of other aspects of the business and this can reduce the focus on winemaking. You get one chance a year to get the wine right and there are all the other employees who depend on that, so the effort has to be put in. I'm reasonably proud of the achievements in the time I was with Angove Family Winemakers. We set out to improve the wines and we did just that. I've always been fond of saying, it's a team thing – it needs everyone's involvement.'

The changes during Warwick's time with Angove Family Winemakers would not have occurred as effectively as they did without considerable investment in new equipment and facilities. Warwick considers that John Angove 'made some very good calls. John does things and you think, "I probably wouldn't have done that." You sit back and watch and it works out – that's experience. He wisely spent a lot of money in changing the bottling hall, a good long-term investment. One of the last things that Jane Gilham bought was a dissolved-oxygen meter. There was quite a lot of head-scratching – why do we need this?

Well, it was one of our biggest problems quality-wise. It's expensive, half the size of a shoebox but costs $25,000. There was some agonising by the Board as to why we needed it. But it was things like this that were massively good investments. John likes to embrace the technology when he sees the point, and that's good.'

Embracing technology, Warwick considered, was probably a family trait. 'Tom was definitely onto technology early on. I could easily have said he was an engineer if I hadn't known he was a qualified winemaker.'

Warwick had seven vintages with Angove Family Winemakers. He decided to move on to other things and he finished up at Christmas 2008. It had been a period of huge change, in the vineyard, in the winemaking processes and the wines the company was producing. 'The winery changed hugely in my time there. They had been a self-reliant business and were now going out and seeing what others were doing, which is how the Australian wine industry has always worked.'

With Warwick's departure, initially back to the world of cider making, Tony Ingle became Senior Winemaker. English-born Tony initially pursued a career in finance. He worked for Japanese and American merchant banks before he embarked on a drastic career change. It was a trip to California and Australia in 1990 that sparked his passion for wine and he spent time in the retail wine trade in the U.K. Through contacts he made in the retail trade, he participated in his first vintage at Chapel Down Winery in East Sussex. He went on to do vintages in France and throughout Australia before moving with his family to Renmark in February 1998 to work as assistant winemaker at Renmano Wines.

After a second vintage in the south of France, Tony commenced study at the University of Adelaide for a Graduate Diploma in Oenology. In October 2002 Tony left Berri Estates and moved to Angove in time for his fifteenth vintage.

'Some big changes were occurring. John Angove took over as Chairman of the Board and Tim Boydell in the sales area. There has been a big change in our winemaking philosophy; we now always aim to do the very best we can. It was difficult to make that change in the first

couple of years – it meant going that extra step. John took control and created a new image for what the company could be. There was a change of feeling in the company, the ability to do.

'We made some interesting wines in 2003. The styles were different and we were selecting parcels of fruit from particular sections of our vineyard. In effect, we were telling Nick Bakkum what to do in his vineyard! This was not how things normally happened. It was a big change, a mental shift, in just two years, but it has worked.'

To what does Tony attribute the leap in wine quality and market success in recent years? 'We are allowing the grapes to show themselves. It is a basic change in winemaking philosophy. Previously, we would try to fix things. If we get good fruit into the winery, the wine really makes itself, we don't have to do anything much to it. It's a key to good winemaking, knowing when to – or not to – intervene.

Although recent changes have been critical in repositioning Angove Family Winemakers, Tony gives due credit to past decisions. 'Tom Angove was visionary when he planted Nanya Vineyard. He picked the right varieties. There were 24 varieties when I joined the company. A few varieties have been removed and of those, the only one I regret losing is Barbera. We have good growers supplying us with some of the newer varieties – Tempranillo, Verdelho, Pinot Gris and Viognier.

'We also have a valuable asset in the 1946 vintage house, designed and built by Tom Angove. We use it for some of our very best wines. There's a story there as to why those wines are so good and how we made them. At the top end our wines are unique and special, not just a commodity. It's what I see as joining business and emotion, one of the reasons I got into winemaking in the first place.'

Tony also saw the move into producing organic wines as important for the company. 'Warwick and I both had a passion to do this. Once the purpose was recognised the company moved quite quickly in this direction. Since 2004 we have been part of the industry's viticultural sustainability charter. I saw the organic move as part of our survival, primarily improving our vineyard health. We need to get back to looking at the vines, not just travelling past them.

'Wine is not just a business. You have to have a passion and want to do it. Organic wine is just another part of that; you just have to work a bit harder, take more care and as a result the wines are better.'

Changes in how Angove Family Winemakers grow their grapes have reaped rewards. 'Nick [Bakkum] really understands the sophistications of viticulture. We spend ages in the vineyard prior to harvest tasting grapes, identifying parcels of fruit for specific purposes. Integration across the whole business is important. If you bring the sales people into the vineyard and the winery they become different people. It gives them the chance to see what goes on, but also to be part of the passion which gives them pride in what we – the company – are doing.'

Changes in winemaking processes

'The way we process fruit and make wine has been transformed. We've moved to a higher plane and that reflects progress in the industry as a whole.' John Angove continued, 'My father [Tom Angove] was very inclined to find his own way to do things – that was his nature. There were established ways to separate juice from skins but he did it his own way. I guess we've moved more back to the standards of the industry rather than having special, unique ways of doing things. It makes it easier for winemakers coming into the winery – they know, rather than having to ask, "How does that work?"'

New crushers and receival bins of greater capacity have been installed. John commented, 'Crushers have improved substantially over the past 10–15 years in their capacity to deal with mechanically harvested fruit and all the other stuff the harvester from time to time wants to put in with the grapes. We prefer good, clean fruit but every now and then you get the load from hell. This can do a lot of damage to machinery, very quickly.

John's view is that, 'We don't see the company making ever increasing volumes of wine, but rather the focus is on making the best we can and to get a better return for what we produce.'

In July 2009 the company installed a Della Toffola cross-flow filtration unit. Cross-flow filtration has been used in the wine industry for many years, but over the last five years significant refinements have seen the technology embraced by wine producers throughout Australia. Experience within the industry has shown that the complete clarification of a wine can be accomplished with only one handling which results in increased finished wine yields, lower labour costs, no wine downgrade through multiple filtration steps and lower generation of waste.

Keeping up with winery technology and equipment can be costly. As John observed, 'The desire for capital expenditure is never ending, but the aim is to just keep ahead of the demand curve.'

Winery operations

Shane Clohesy was appointed in the role of Winery Services Manager in January 2003 after 24 years of experience in vineyards and winemaking. This was a period of evolution in the winemaking area of the company. It was decided that there was a need

Vintage scenes, Renmark Winery –

Top left: Annabelle Evans, Winemaker.
Opposite: Cindy McDonald, Laboratory
Technician

Centre left: Senior Winemaker
Tony Ingle with John Angove

Bottom left: Winemaking team 2010 –
Rear (L to R): Paul Kernich, Tony Ingle,
Alex Russell, Danai Ioannidou,
Shane Clohesy. Front (L to R):
Stacey Sheppard, Ben Horley

Bottom centre: former Senior
Winemaker Warwick Billings

Centre right: Senior Cellar Hands –
(L to R): James Gibson, Steve Tillett,
Bill Palat

Top right: Shane Clohesy,
Winery Services Manager

to have two Senior Winemakers and a Production Manager to facilitate the increased focus on fine wine production which was increasing dramatically. Shane said, 'My experience in winemaking could assist the winemakers – I would do the paperwork and they could concentrate on the winemaking. I also deal with bulk wine sales and the contract bottling. I book the vintage, make sure things flow. We would struggle to do that without someone dedicated to the task. Overall, we are about consistency and continual improvement.'

Guided by sales and marketing, the operations team organises to purchase what is needed for production. Shane said, 'My role is to pull a lot of things together. At vintage, the winemakers, Nick Bakkum and I work out the schedule and what we're going to make from what fruit. In essence, efficiency is required to get as much through the winery as we can to minimise costs. Quality is all about getting the grapes into the winery in the best condition and getting the wine out in the best condition. You can't increase the quality of poor material.

'Warwick Billings and Tony Ingle have done a tremendous job in producing consistently good quality wines. Consistency is very important in a brand. Because of the quality, we're now in the position where we can sell everything we make.'

Maintenance

Historically, Angove Family Winemakers had a full in-house maintenance team. They had most skills available to maintain all aspects of winery operations. Although the number of maintenance people has been reduced, the company probably still has more than other similar sized operations. Greater use is now made of external contractors.

The Works Manager/Maintenance Planner, Neale Dunhill, joined Angove in 1977 and has come up through the business. He left for a brief period but returned in 1992. He commenced as an apprentice welder making stainless steel storage tanks. At that time there were over 25 maintenance people employed on-site. Currently they have 6–8. But having said that, Neale remarked, 'You have to remember that then most of the buildings were of timber and corrugated galvanised iron; very few had any steel in them. We had a team of painters to maintain the buildings.'

Neale's role has developed over time. He spent 10 years in charge of the civil department during which time he was involved in a variety of projects including design work. He prepared site drawings locating everything on the site, 'it's a very useful management tool'. His present role includes managing the daily work program and record-keeping for various national and international quality standards with which the company complies.

Maintenance group March 2010 –
Rear: John Green, Clarke Schober, Shane Pitman, Andrew Webb. Front: Neale Dunhill, Mike Telling, Travis Gates

Shane Pitman joined Angove in March 2001 while Andrew Darby was Operations Manager. On Andrew's departure, Shane stepped into the key role of Maintenance Manager reporting to the new General Manager Operations, Jim Godden.

Environmental management

The way wineries deal with the waste they generate has changed dramatically over recent decades.

Environmental management at Angove Family Winemakers has been under the direction of Jim Godden since 2007. Jim took up the position of General Manager Operations after being in a similar role with Hardy Wine Company at Berri and prior to that with an international petroleum company. Environmental management is just one of his responsibilities in managing winery and allied services for the company. He provides support and long-term planning for various areas of winery operation.

Prior to Jim becoming General Manager Operations, the role was divided between the Production Manager (winemaking based) and Operations Manager (wine bottling and maintenance). When the Operations Manager, Andrew Darby, left, it was decided to combine some of the responsibilities in a new position of General Manager Operations with the Production Manager mainly overseeing the winemaking side of the business.

Jim is proud of the company's environmental management which he sees as a fundamental component of handing on the business in good condition to the next generation. Although Angove has at times been ahead of what have been the legal requirements, Jim suggested that consumers did not see environmental issues as fashionable or important. Apart from that, Angove have generally not publicised what they do in this area.

Legislative requirements have changed how wineries operate, especially in the area of waste disposal. As Jim observed, 'There is now common recognition of the impact we as a community have on our environment. As such, we are licenced for the activities we undertake. We're in a semi-rural area and near what used to be a creek, and we create waste in our processes. The general attitude 40 years ago was that you just put your waste over there – in or on the ground, in the water – it just went away. Now the drivers are reuse and recycle – minimise the impact of your waste.'

Wastewater management is an important focus of the company's environmental responsibilities. It is derived from various winery processes. Between 2003 and 2010, Angove reduced their generation of wastewater by 50–60%. As Jim Godden observed, 'Less water is being used but we need to be careful, at the same time, not to over-concentrate the waste as you end up with another type of disposal problem. Some of the chemicals we use are caustic and this waste cannot be directly disposed of onto land for the water to evaporate. Some chemical wastes need to be treated prior to disposal to change the chemical composition of the waste.'

Angove disposes of wastewater to an 8-ha woodlot of River Red Gums. The woodlot was developed by Don Lill who worked with Angove for 22 years, from 1980 until 2002. Jim Godden related, 'Don had a fruit block at Renmark and was very interested in growing native plants. He set up the woodlot; the area was a degraded saltpan at the time. It now attracts a lot of small birds, as well as kangaroos and emus. The creek, as we call it, is actually a constructed disposal drain for intercepted saline irrigation water. By planting River Red Gums, we have provided habitat and amenity, and a treed environment.'

'The waste is mostly low in nutrients and BOD [biological oxygen demand] varies with the season of the year. This water is untreated, except for pH adjustment, and is used on the woodlot. Cleaner wastewater streams, from the bottling plant and the centrifuges is treated through a cross-flow filter and is stored in tanks for reuse on our gardens and lawns. Rainwater is harvested from the buildings and we can store around 200,000 L on-site at any time. We also treat River Murray water but this process only cuts in when the supply of rainwater falls below a critical level.

Prior to developing the wastewater processes, there was limited environmental management in place. Works Manager Neale Dunhill commented, 'The company quickly became leaders in the field and it was an exciting time to be involved. We were forward thinking in putting this system in place and it was more than was required by the authorities. We were probably 5–10 years ahead of where most companies were at.'

Greenhouse gas emissions have become a strong environmental focus for the company in recent years. The company is not in the tier of business where they legally have to report on emissions but there is an agreement with the wine industry on a State-level for wineries to record their Carbon footprint. Jim Godden said, 'If we do that we can start to reduce it. Regardless of the arguments regarding global warming, this has made us focus on doing the best for our environment.'

Jim sees Angove Family Winemakers' strength in the environmental area as developing the ability to demonstrate that their operations are sustainable. 'Sustainability is not an easy parameter to demonstrate but documentation and monitoring of what we do is critical. It's about mapping your business, understanding your business and identifying the risk factors and minimising them.

'It takes a lot of time to set up a full business management system and run the reporting but it is of critical benefit to a successful business which is what we are all about.'

Water use and recycling is an important part of Angove's environmental management programme. Most wastewater from the winery is treated and reused; the balance is disposed to an 8 hectare woodlot of River Red Gums. The site was previously a degraded salt scald.

Purchasing and packaging

Bottling office staff, March 2010 –
L to R: Sonnie Hand, Michael Walters, Rita Richardson,
Alison Phillips, Nicole Vallelonga, Grant Armstrong,
Jim Godden, Brad Yarwood

For many years the purchasing and packaging area was under the management of Gienus Doevendans. Gienus joined Angove straight from school in 1965. He did various jobs in his early years, including that of Junior Storeman working with Cyril Brady. After a few years he went in to the office as a clerk dealing with purchase orders and liaising with the sales people. The team comprised 3 or 4 sales people but Angove also sold wine through agents such as Elders. Gienus recalled, 'I spent one week a month visiting grocery stores in Melbourne. Stores bought wine in bulk and decanted it into flagons for their customers. I also arranged for a truck to take bulk wine to northern Queensland every month or so. The wine went in hogsheads and quarter casks. I would fly to Queensland once a year to visit storekeepers.'

Gienus did an accounting course, part-time over seven years. He introduced a stock card system to keep track of dry goods stocks and this was used up until the first electronic accounting process was introduced. Cyril Brady retired in 1983 and Gienus took on the role of Purchasing Manager. In addition to the purchase of the major consumables – bottles, corks, cartons, labels – he also dealt with the purchase of grapes. He no longer visits the growers as the company's grower liaison officers discuss a whole range of matters with their growers, including grape production practices and quality control.

In his early days, liaising with growers was more about volume than quality. Angove was mainly buying Doradillo, Sultana, Trebbiano and Palomino for brandy and fortified wine production. Gienus recalled, 'Initially most of the growers were Australians by birth but the region gradually saw more of the vineyards taken over by European and Asian families. They have worked hard and have expanded their vineyards to give their children opportunities they did not have. There have been difficult years – the growers need to feed their families but we may not have a market for the wine. We try to do what we can and many growers have remained loyal to the company for a long, long time.'

Gienus managed the bottling line for five years and saw the output potential increase from about 250,000 dozen to 1.3 million dozen per annum. He left this role a couple of years before the new bottling line was installed in 2004. He then managed the company's purchasing and packaging department; he is also a member of the Company's Board of Directors.

Bottling and shipping

The new bottling facility and contract bottling

In 2004 Angove Family Winemakers commissioned a new bottling facility. It was a bold, and expensive, decision to take but it has enabled the company to have complete control over the bottling of their own wines and to undertake contract wine bottling for other companies.

As John Angove related, 'We had bottling capacity and equipment and machinery that was adequate, quite sophisticated, doing a good job, but it was housed in an environment that was not suited to meet the demands of quality audited standards that we wanted to achieve.'

According to former Operations Manager, Andrew Darby, the original bottling line needed an overhaul. 'We probably outgrew the bottling hall in a number of ways five or so years before it was replaced. It was a bit of a chicken and egg issue; do you replace it and then find the business, or do you find the business first and then replace the line. Both approaches have their dangers.

'It was decided to replace the bottling facility. It was the single largest capital expenditure for the company for a long time and involved outlaying a lot of money over a short period of time. It was a big project for me to head and for the company to fund. I approached it with a couple of things in mind. Firstly, to secure the food standards needed to ensure us to continue to export wine, and secondly, to offer the opportunity for the company to undertake contract bottling to provide it with another income stream. We achieved both goals.

'The project spanned around 12 months. It was very much a team effort – all parties put in their requirements. It was a huge task.

'Before starting the project, Gienus Doevendans, Claude Sarti [former bottling manager] and I visited a number of bottling plants. They all suffered from a lack of space and the line had to twist and turn to fit into the available space. This was less than ideal. We had the luxury of space at the winery site and a straight line is ideal.

'The outer shell of the new building was developed and the equipment was moved in. Some parts of the project offered greater challenges than others but we got there on time. Getting the network of gas, water, wine and power lines connected to the facility was pretty complicated. We had pages and pages of scale drawings. As it turned out, we had nothing worse than a few pipes missing by a millimetre or so, which was pretty good. We ran the first case of wine off the new line at 10 pm on the night before our expected (or hoped for) completion date.'

The Hon. Kaylene Maywald MP officially opened the new facility on 28 May 2004.

On the new facility, John Angove observed, 'Comment has been made, "You are setting the benchmark for wine bottling in Australia at the moment." Maybe it's not the fastest production line but certainly the standard of the facility is very, very high. It has been responsible for getting some of the contract bottling we currently have. The response from potential customers is that "I think we can rely on these people to get it right." It has also had a bearing on some of the overseas links we have established. They've come, had a look around and have decided *we're happy with what we see.*'

Andrew Darby left Angove in 2006 after 21 years with the company. 'It was a hard decision to take but it was time to move on to other things. There were some challenges, which you need from time to time, but they were good years.'

> The bottling plant – If both lines operate five days a week, two shifts per day (total of 15 hours), in theory, Angove can put out 3.6 million dozen cases per annum. However, as General Manager Operations Jim Godden comments, 'Various downtimes make that impossible for us to achieve. In the financial year 2009 we packed 10.2 million litres or 1.12 million cases (9 L equivalents) – so, there's obviously still scope to increase our output.'

Contract bottling now contributes substantially to the business. As Company Secretary Andrew Coombe commented, 'We have been able to offer this service because we now have a world-standard bottling facility, operating to British Retail Consortium (BRC) standards, one of the highest ratings in the world.' Winemaking Services Manager Shane Clohesy observes, 'Contract bottling has really taken off in the past four years. With the downturn in export sales, we weren't bottling as much of our own wine as in past years, so the contract work has filled the gap. We have some big customers and we have not had to look for business. We advertise by producing a very good end product and people get to know this. Our brokerage firms have us at the top of their list as being a good firm to deal with for bottling.'

General Manager Operations Jim Godden attributes a great deal of the success of the contract bottling to the dedication of those people who work on the line. 'It's critical to maintain the highest of standards at all times and the bottling team do just that. We have a very dedicated team who are committed to producing a quality product the first time and every time.'

John Angove and daughter Victoria, 2006

19 Angove Family Winemakers

In a dramatic change with the past, the company was rebranded in 2007. The change from *Angove's* to *Angove Family Winemakers* took several years to bring to fruition but it has been well-received by the wine trade and consumers alike.

A driving force behind the change was General Manager Sales and Marketing Tim Boydell who had been directing changes in sales and marketing. Tim joined Angove in 1999 in a wine export role. His previous role was in marketing with another family-owned company, S. Smith & Sons. Tim soon showed aptitudes and drive for extra responsibilities. He was appointed as General Manager Sales and Marketing and in November 2002 was invited to join the Company's Board.

Tim commented, 'When I first joined the Company and went travelling around, we were very much regarded as a Riverland wine company. So, the goal was to make a paradigm shift. Our research showed that we were not well-known, at least not by the name Angove. We were known for the products we sold. The rebranding of the company and associated changes were massive undertakings. However, it was a very useful process that we went through.'

John Angove's daughter, Victoria, joined Angove in 2001 (see Chapter 20) and from the outset supported Tim in his push to rebrand the Company. She reflected, 'Tim saw the importance of *family* in marketing our wines. We are modern and contemporary but we also have the tradition of a family business behind us.'

A decade ago the company was promoting the sub-brands of their wines – Butterfly Ridge, Classic Reserve, Sarnia Farm, for example – and not the name *Angove*. As Matt Redin (National Marketing Manager) observed, 'The *Angove* brand name was poorly recognised by consumers because of this. The first move was to increase the font size of Angove on the label. Then, in exploring the possible changes that ultimately lead to the adoption of the name Angove Family Winemakers, Tim Boydell introduced the tag line, '5 Generations of Winemaking Excellence' to the labelling. This was a good start but it did not tell the whole story.'

The impetus for further changes occurred when John Angove and his wife, Claire, were at the Vancouver Playhouse Wine Festival in 2006. As John related, 'Australia was the focus country for the festival that year. There were lots of brands there. As you walked in, there was Bethany Wines – Schrapel Family Vineyards, Brown Brothers, D'Arenberg McLaren Vale and *Angove's*. It was so blunt and cold; I thought we just had to do something about it.'

Richard, John and Victoria Angove outside the company's offices at Renmark, 2010

Various options were considered but none got the support of the advertising people. Any further action was shelved for a while and a year later Victoria Angove and Tim Boydell felt that they should look at it once again. John Angove related, 'We started a project with Tucker Design; they went right back to the name, the crest, our history and came up with various options, including *Angove Family Winemakers since 1886*.'

'Angove Family Winemakers was adopted. *Angove Family* brings people into the equation, *Winemakers* describes the business and *since* 1886 indicates continuity since that date. Tucker Design then worked on the design for our labels. The family crest featuring a double-headed eagle had been widely used on the packaging since the 1970s but is now used more sparingly and is reserved for our premium wines. There has been good, strong response from the market to the new naming and designs.'

Tim Boydell and Matt Redin strongly supported the changes. Tim commented, 'The rebranding of the company was a massive undertaking. However, it was a wonderful process that we went through and, I think, because it was so rigorous in its formality and structure, as we went along it reinforced that we were on the right track. The market research we did [in September 2007] showed that although we thought we were doing well and were recognised, the reality was that we weren't well-known, at least by the name *Angove*. We were known for the products that we sold – names like St Agnes, Marko Vermouth and Stone's Green Ginger. People could clearly recognise us once we pointed out the products we sold but otherwise, we weren't well-known at all.' Matt Redin agreed, 'Less than 10 years ago we were promoting our sub-brands, not Angove. We were not telling people who we were and there was no obvious correlation for consumers between St Agnes and Angove.'

According to John Angove, 'My father always saw Angove as the family name and something private. He always sought an overarching brand but never found one that worked. Our label names were line names, not a brand name. To establish that is really hard – but, in effect we already have it in *Angove* but we had not used it in that way.'

However, Matt Redin observed, 'This lack of recognition could have been seen as a negative but it also meant we could start afresh with open eyes to what we want to achieve. So, we've emphasised the company's heritage, since 1886; Angove Family Winemakers says it all very plainly. We had the family story and it's a real story, a family company, not a dreamed up story, and we have the products.'

Having quality wines has been critical to the success of the relabelling. Huge changes have occurred in how the company produces its fine wines. 'We have restructured the winemaking side of the business', said Matt Redin. It's common in wine companies for the approach to be *here's some wine, put it in a bottle, and now sell it*. Our approach has become, we need a wine to fit this price point and style, here's the type of packaging, can you make a wine to that level? We've almost turned the process around and we've become market-driven based on what we know our consumers – the market – want. Our winemakers in recent years, Warwick Billings and Tony Ingle, have been instrumental in changing how we do things. There have also been big changes in how we grow our grapes and now there's great cooperation between those people growing the grapes and those making the wine. We're getting accolades and awards for our wines and this adds another dimension to the story we can tell.'

John, Victoria and Richard Angove, March 2011

20 The fifth generation

A custodian in the line

Maintaining Angove Family Winemakers as an independent, family-owned company has been important to both Tom and John Angove. When asked, over 20 years ago, if he had been made offers to sell the company, Tom Angove indicated that he had but quickly added that he had no intention of selling, saying, 'If I did sell, what would I do?' The winery was Tom's pride and joy for all of his working life.

Operating a private family company does provide its owners with more freedom to plan for the long-term without having continually to appease shareholders, but it does present its own challenges. Owners can feel that they have a major personal responsibility to safeguard their family's investment for future generations and for the well-being of their employees and the community in which they operate.

John Angove married junior-primary schoolteacher Claire Sanderson on 18 January 1975, and they have three children, Victoria, Richard and Sophie.

John says that his attitude to the family company changed when the children were growing up. 'As they have got older it has further changed my view of the winery just as a place to work to being a place of work and, yes, maybe one day the children might take an interest. Now, in fact, they are heavily involved, and literally, I have to keep this place going so that they can have something to take over. I'm really just a custodian in the line.'

Few family companies survive into the fifth generation. John Angove considers one of the reasons for Angove continuing to be a successful family company has been 'a fairly thin line of succession'. He continued, 'We have not had major internal family problems to resolve. One of my father's great achievements was to collect up the small parcels of shares that my grandfather handed out in return for long and loyal service.'

The opening of the Angove Still House at the Hickinbotham Roseworthy Wine Science Laboratory at the Waite Campus of the University of Adelaide in 2003 – (L to R): John, Richard and Victoria Angove (University of Adelaide)

By his actions, Tom Angove 'established the security of the company from a corporate ownership point of view, so that it can continue because of the way we have set up the ownership structure. Added to this, of course, is the need to remain finacially viable.'

John recognises the importance of proper succession planning to enable the transition from one generation to the next to occur as smoothly as possible. He has encouraged his family to be involved in the business, if they chose to be, and also to learn a critical understanding of the wine industry from external sources. 'Not only does this bring to the company the benefits of outside experience and knowledge, but it ensures that the family members who come into the business are fully committed to the cause. I like to think that this is one of the reasons for the company's success.'

Enter the next generation

The last decade has seen two of John and Claire's children, Victoria and Richard, come into the family business. Whilst Claire has not worked in the family company in any formal sense, she has contributed substantially from behind the scenes. 'I enjoyed teaching and for that reason went back once the children were at secondary school. Teaching gave me a degree of flexibility to support John in his role in the business. I've travelled extensively with John to visit our overseas markets and to promote Angove wines, including conducting wine tastings at events and promotions.'

Victoria and John Angove on the bottling line, Renmark Winery, 2006

She has watched with interest the changes in the company in recent years and the recognition that their wines are now receiving. 'We have great employees, very dedicated people. John doesn't micro-manage people. He knows the direction the company needs to go and he gives people the room to make decisions and get on with the job at hand. The company has a good mixture of being both conservative and progressive in what we do.

'The new labelling is a good example of this. The wording describes who we are and what we do. The design and lettering are smart and modern, and the continued use of the family crest is an important link with the company's heritage.'

Claire is both pleased and proud that the next generation are now actively involved in the business. Their joining the company occurred in quite different ways.

Victoria Angove was educated at Renmark and in Adelaide, at Woodlands Church of England Girls' Grammar School. In 1993 she was named South Australian Young Achiever of the Year and went on to be a National Finalist in the Young Achiever of the Year Awards.

From a very young age, Victoria was actively interested in the family's winery and 'wine business' at large. 'My interest has always been in the workings of the business. I like wine and appreciate it, but have never been interested in winemaking as such. During school and university holidays, we were encourage to learn about the various aspects of the business; working on the bottling line, in administration, the winery and despatch. Our parents took great care in encouraging us to pursue all areas of interest, not wanting any of us to feel 'obliged' to enter the family business.'

Victoria completed a Bachelor of Commerce degree at the University of Adelaide in 1997, with double majors in Marketing and Management. She then headed to Canada to work in a snow ski resort and a white-water rafting company. After a year of backpacking, home (and a lack of finances) began calling and she returned to Adelaide to a temporary sales representative position at Angove.

At the beginning of 2000, with the sales representative contract completed, Victoria took up a position as a coordinator at the International Wine and Spirit Challenge in London. Working there she gained a solid understanding of the extent of the wine and spirit trade in the world, and its staggering diversity. 'It was a great exposure to wines from all over the world, an intensive learning environment. Over the six months, my fascination with the wine business grew stronger, but my love for the English climate did not. I commenced travelling through the Mediterranean, visiting Greece, Italy, France and Spain and many of their grape growing and winemaking regions. I spent time in Spain, attempting to learn Spanish and working in a winery just south of Barcelona.'

At the end of 2000, she returned home to Australia, happy to lock up her backpack. She worked at Angove as a cellar hand during the 2001 vintage, keen to learn further about the production side of the business before commencing in the Sales and Marketing Department. 'It was an interesting time. I was probably the first female to work in the cellar. The winemaker, Jane Gilham, said, "They will make it tough for you and I don't want you to fail." It was a great opportunity to see what occurs on the floor. Surviving that was a great accomplishment and it gave me an understanding that I wouldn't other-wise have.'

With the company undergoing rapid development in Sales and Marketing, Victoria became understudy to Tim Boydell and was given the responsibility for exports to Europe and Asia as one of the company's Regional Export Managers. When Angove appointed a UK export manager, Victoria focused on Asia and the United States of America. 'With the development of our association with Trinchero Family Estates came a real renewal of interest in the USA market and I spent a lot more time in the market there. As a member of the family, I actively participated in public relations domestically and overseas with a particular focus on the burgeoning USA market.'

Victoria's activities in Asia saw the company add many new countries to its distri-bution base, including China, India, Sri Lanka and Vietnam, whilst developing their existing business throughout the region. 'The Asian market has since become a full-time role. Every country there is different, both culturally and in its legal requirements. China now has a very sophisticated wine market. Japan has always been so with lots of wines from France, Spain and Italy sold there.

'Being young and female didn't help me in some of the Asian markets but being an Angove did, not that it's something I've ever traded on. It was important to them that they were dealing with a member of the Angove family in purchasing our wines rather than dealing with someone who they may feel is an outsider.'

Seeking further challenges, Victoria relocate to Sydney in 2004 to work with the National Sales Manager in the management of the company's business with National Accounts, namely Woolworths and Coles Myer liquor chains.

Following the resignation of her aunt, Frances Angove, Victoria was appointed to the Company's Board of Directors in December 2006.

Victoria returned to Adelaide in June 2008 with her husband, Heath Amber, just prior to taking maternity leave. She returned to work in October 2009 in a business development role. She says she has had some good teachers over her years in the family business, especially Tim Boydell, Matt Redin and her father. 'My father has taught me the importance of patience; it is something that needs to be learnt. He has made some very good decisions to take the company to where we are now and for the recognition we are now getting. I remember asking him, when I was about 15, how he would make a decision. I was interested in his thought process and how he worked things through. He said he uses our mission statement as his guide. "If I make the decision this way, will it go towards our mission? If not, it's not the right way to go." It's a very good discipline in making important decisions.'

Whereas Victoria's passion lies in the area of business and management, her brother's has been in winemaking. Richard made his first wine when he was about seven. As Victoria recalled, 'We had a small vineyard near our house. Dad and Richard made some wine using baker's yeast. It was quite drinkable, I think.'

Richard first worked at the winery when he was 15, packing export containers. The cartons of wine were stacked by hand into the container and, as he recalls, 'it got very hot inside the container'. He also did cellar work during the summer school holidays and in 2000 did his first vintage, mainly in the red wine area. He completed a Business Degree at the University of South Australia and then a Post Graduate degree in Oenology at the University of Adelaide's Waite Campus in 2003. Up until this time, Richard was more interested in working as a snow ski instructor, but as Victoria said, 'When he did the winemaking course, it was as if a light was switched on. He went from being interested in wine to extraordinarily passionate, captivated by it, and what's more, he has an incredible palate.'

He then went to the USA and did vintage work in the Napa Valley in California. Returning to Australia, he took a 12-week vintage contract position at Brokenwood Wines in the Hunter Valley and ended up remaining there on and off for four years. He did the 2006 vintage at Brown Brothers at Milawa, in north-eastern Victoria. He found it a great experience working in a company of this size and making 'very technically sophisticated wines from fruit coming from a variety of districts in Victoria.'

The following vintage he went back to Brokenwood Wines and then took a position with McPherson Wines at Nagambie on the Goulburn River, Victoria. He did two vintages there, finishing in March 2008 and then did a vintage at Tamar Ridge Wines in Tasmania. By now Richard felt that he 'had enough experience to come back to South Australia and had something to offer the family company'.

In 2008 he was appointed Brand Manager with responsibility for the company's agency portfolio. 'The company's agencies had grown considerably over the past five years. Matt Redin had been handling this area as well as his other responsibilities and it was felt he could do with some assistance to manage the agency lines.'

The first year was 'lots of learning on the job' and helping the role to evolve. 'It's important to have good contact and reporting systems with our agency companies. We jointly work out budgeting for advertising and promoting their wines. We are also looking for further opportunities in this area of the business – where are the gaps in our portfolio, nichés that we can fill, and where can we enhance product offering?'

Outside of his role in Angove, Richard has become involved in Wine Show judging. 'I did lots of tasting at Brokenwood, including masked wines. You soon start seeing regional differences and styles. I did the Advanced Wine Assessment Course at the Australian Wine Research Institute in 2007. We looked at 150 wines over four days.

Richard Angove at Nanya Vineyard

They analyse your results to see how consistent you are over time. I was an Associate Judge at the Victorian Wine Show and was then invited to judge at the Adelaide Wine Show in September 2008. That was fairly daunting; a lot of wines over four-and-a half days, but it was a really good forum to see what wines are out there in the marketplace and then to assess our wines against them.' He was an Associate Judge at Adelaide again in 2009 and 2010.

Victoria and Richard's sister Sophie has chosen a different career path than her siblings. John Angove commented, 'Sophie, is a supporter of the industry as a consumer. She has not as yet shown a strong interest in the business but at odd times has been involved in events and has been sensational. We had a group of Canadian visitors in Renmark for an introductory exercise. There would have been a dozen of them and part of the program was to have them at our home. They came down by river; they skied and swam and came to the house for dinner. Sophie got involved in that event. She drove the boat for the skiing and had dinner with us. Nick, the manager of the Canadian company said, "You can send Sophie to help us promote any time you like".'

Sophie became very involved in the field of autism, in particular, teaching autistic children in Adelaide. She completed her Masters in Special Education in June 2009. During 2010 she commenced a Science degree in environmental management, a fore-runner to a career change.

The end of an era

Tom Angove retired as Chairman of the Board of Angove's Pty Ltd in 2001. After an active life in the wine business, retirement did not come easily to Tom. He always had some project or other to work on, even if it was just 'tinkering around' or 'fixing things' in his well-equipped workshop at *Terragong*. At the time of his retirement, he described survival of the family company as his

The comment 'he should have been an engineer' comes up quite often when Tom Angove's career is discussed. John Angove commented, 'His focus on building the infrastructure of the winery from the mid-1940s onwards was his greatest love. Yet, he only ever described it as *his collection of tin sheds*.'

greatest achievement and this at a time when many well-known family wine companies were being sold or absorbed by large overseas interests. Tom's was a life full of achievements but he remained a modest, private man, never seeking recognition or the limelight, in fact, he was reluctant to accept that he had actually earned any of the recognitions that he was given.

Working was Tom's joy and, as the family found, 'the word holiday was not strong in his vocabulary'. However, as John recalled, 'Without doubt the best week in his year was around the full moon in June when he would get together four or five friends and disappear up the River Murray on his houseboat 'Ibis' to duck shoot, fish, rest and unwind. I remember Bob Abbott, Tom's right-hand man at work for 40 years, saying that if you had a serious issue to raise with TW that could cause major problems, then, if you wanted a good outcome, just after a week up the river was always a good time to tackle it.'

Tom loved family outings on the river, water-skiing (his speed boat was creatively named *Whiz Bang*), and flying his plane. He was well-known for his particular interest in words and English expression. When he decided it was time to withdraw from industry organisations he cited 'the coming of inevitable decrepitude' as his reason. His health deteriorated in his final years but he retained a strong interest in his family and the company. As John Angove commented, 'His determination to build the company and establish it as a serious player within the Australian wine industry was a driving force in his life. He strongly believed that no-one achieves in isolation and said that those around him were a critical part of the whole. Bob Abbott, Bill Marshall, Bill Crowe, Ken Stevens, Cyril Brady, Bob Hill and Stan Sheppard were vital parts of the jigsaw and their input and commitment was recognised and greatly appreciated.'

Tom Angove was, as his grand-daughter Victoria said, 'A man of great courage and determination, who had so many areas of interest, so many things he was passionate about and who worked so hard to excel in these areas.' Tom died at Renmark on 30 March 2010 aged 92. A memorial service was held at *Terragong* in the garden he loved so much overlooking the great River Murray.

Tom Angove, 1997.
Photo courtesy The Advertiser

Angove premium wines

With the changes that have occurred since 2002, the Angove range of wines has further evolved. Some labels have been discontinued – Sarnia Farm, Classic Reserve, Stonegate, Misty Mooring – and new ones introduced including Vineyard Select, Nine Vines, Bear Crossing, Chalk Hill Blue and Brightlands. Greater emphasis is being placed on bottled fine wines reflecting the trend in the industry across the Australian (and overseas) markets. Industry figures show that overall bottled wines have increased from 34.1% of the market in 1993–1994 to 53.7% in 2008–2009; during the same period the market share of soft packs (wine cask) fell from 66.9% to 44.6% (AWBC Annual Reports).

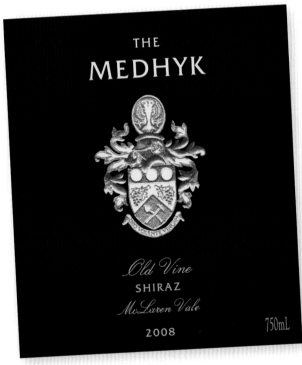

The Medhyk

The Medhyk 2008 McLaren Vale Old Vine Shiraz was first released in May 2011 to commemorate 125 years of wine-making by the Angove family in South Australia. Medhyk is Cornish for doctor and the wine was named in honour of the company's founder, Dr William T. Angove, a Cornish-born medical practitioner. The fruit was selected from three distinguished sites on the gentle slopes of McLaren Vale; the vines ranging from 40 to over 60 years of age and producing less than 1.5 tonnes per acre of extraordinarily high quality fruit.

The fruit was bunch sorted prior to crushing and the must was chilled and kept at 5°C for five days before a gentle warming and fermenting. Half way through ferment any unbroken grapes were crushed using the age-old method of piégeage [entrapment]. Once the alcoholic fermentation had finished the wine remained on skins under inert gas protection until the wine had extracted complex tannins from the skins and seeds. A small wooden basket press was used to gently extract the full flavour of the wine which was then aged in 100% new French oak barrels. A secondary fermentation was completed prior to a program of racking to clarify the wine. After two years in barrel a rigorous selection and blending then took place prior to bottling.

The wine is deep, intense purple in colour and the aromas are typical of the variety and the region. The wine was described by a reviewer as being 'made by learned hands with a deft touch. The wine is rich, deeply-flavoured ... a serious, savoury Shiraz built for the cellar.'

Vineyard Select

For their range of premium hand-crafted fine wines Angove has sourced grapes from various grape-growing regions of South Australia. The wines are made in limited quantities and great care is taken to emphasise varietal and regional characteristics. The range now comprises five wines, Coonawarra Cabernet Sauvignon, McLaren Vale Shiraz, Clare Valley Riesling, Mount Benson Chardonnay and Adelaide Hills Sauvignon Blanc.

Sourcing the grapes requires the winemaker and the vineyard manager to visit the contract grower to discuss their needs and nearer to vintage determining when to pick. As former Angove winemaker Warwick Billings said, 'We would go down to Coonawarra, for instance, and say these grapes are ready for picking. That's a six-hour drive from Renmark, each way, so you don't want to have to do it too often, so you need to get on with and trust the people who are growing for you but then you still need to go and make sure because that's what winemakers do. The logistics were not hard really once we established a process.'

In addition to the regions from where the grapes for the Vineyard Select range are sourced, Angove also buy grapes from the South Flinders region, one of the newest grape-growing areas of South Australia. Warwick commented, 'It is a great region with good grapes. We started taking fruit from the region in 2005. It suits the winery very well to

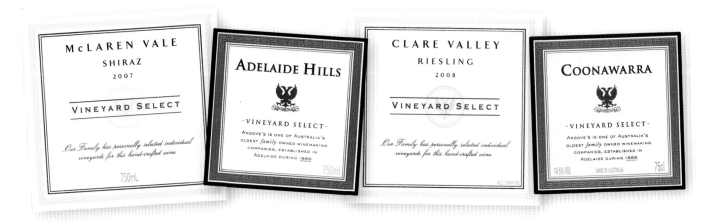

have those grapes because they come in three weeks earlier than any other fruit. Southern Flinders has a good grape-growing environment – soils, rainfall, temperatures, diurnal range, etc. must be right because the grapes are good – black, flavoursome, ripe Shiraz.'

The outstanding quality of the Vineyard Select range has been recognised in wine shows and by wine critics in Australia and internationally. Recent vintages of McLaren Vale Shiraz and Coonawarra Cabernet Sauvignon have consistently scored 88–91 and 87–92 points, respectively, in reviews and have been acclaimed as 'impressive' examples of their region and style and the wines demonstrate 'the quality of the workmanship'. The 2008 Cabernet Sauvignon was awarded Silver Medals at the 2010 Shanghai International Wine Challenge and the 2010 Decanter World Wine Awards.

> The 2006 **Clare Valley Riesling** was 'Wine of the Year' at the Clare Valley Wine Show in 2006. The vintages from 2007 to 2010, received 2 Gold, 6 Silver and 12 Bronze medals at wine shows and scored 88–92 points in reviews. The 2009 vintage was awarded a Gold Medal at the 2010 International Wine Challenge and the 2010 a Gold Medal at the New Zealand Wine Show.

Nine Vines

Chief Winemaker Tony Ingle says of the Nine Vines range, 'Nine Vines is an exciting collection of distinct varieties and styles. We have endeavoured to capture and preserve the vibrant fruit flavours in the grapes and present them in the wines.' If show awards are any reflection, they have achieved this goal. The first wine in the Nine Vines range was introduced in 2003 and there are now six wines under this label – Grenache Shiraz Rosé, Pinot Grigio, Viognier, Moscato, Shiraz Viognier and Tempranillo Shiraz. The range has won great critical acclaim and the Rosé has become Australia's most highly awarded Rosé.

Warwick Billings recalled, 'The range began with the Grenache Shiraz Rosé – we made 1000 cases the first year. The marketing people were a bit sceptical about a Rosé. Tony Ingle started the next vintage and he wanted to make a Rosé, so we gave it a go. He had a good pedigree as a Rosé maker and one of the sales people – Toby Hill – said you could sell good Rosé. We managed to convince everyone else that a Rosé would be a good plan; we made some, a lovely wine, and it all sold. So, the next year we made three times as much. The Nine Vines label was created for the Rosé and it's a good label – we got good feedback. It looks a bit different, quite modern and suits the Rosé well.'

According to Tony Ingle, 'The Rosé is a European style wine – Warwick and I both have that background. Rosé is right for our environment, lower alcohol, savoury and with brilliant colour.' The wine is bright red–pink in colour with clean, fresh flavours and is quite dry.

Angove made the Rosé for three years before they brought out another wine in the range. The second wine was Viognier, then followed Shiraz Viognier, Tempranillo Shiraz, Pinot Grigio (in 2008), and Moscato (2010).

Warwick Billings related, 'The Viognier – the timing wasn't bad and the grapes were available; we were probably a bit self-indulgent as winemakers – we like to do something that is a bit different. When Tony and I first went to see the vineyard, the grapes looked all shrivelled and horrible. It's a strange grape and still not common in Australia. We went to another vineyard to see what their Viognier looked like – it was just like ours! We got the grapes in and fermented them in a fairly European manner. At the tastings, people didn't really like it – however, it's grown on them … Anyway, we had a buyer come out from England and he bought it.

'The Shiraz Viognier – to do it properly you need to put all the grapes in together, it's synergistic – you get darker red wine and it's better if you put the Shiraz grapes into the white juice. It takes a bit of coordinating, but it's a good end result. The Tempranillo Shiraz – we used Tempranillo by itself for a few years but it wasn't going anywhere. We then got a better grower who had quite nice Tempranillo fruit. It was still a bit of a hard sell. The wine can be harsh, not immediately pleasant to the taste.

You don't want to keep it for five years like they do in Spain. I'd just come back from doing a vintage in Spain where we'd been making Tempranillo Shiraz blends. It works better than the straight wine. Our wine was runner-up for a Trophy at the Adelaide Wine Show in 2008.'

For most of the years that Warwick Billings was with Angove Family Winemakers, he spent three months overseas. He comments, 'It was very understanding and far-sighted of John [Angove] to let his Chief Winemaker run off for three months – I feel it contributed to our winemaking knowledge. It was good that I could do that.

'I worked in Italy and made lots of Pinot Grigio. At Angove we made our wine in a similar manner but slightly better, and it all sold.'

Nine Vines highly awarded – The success of the Nine Vines range has been led by 'the stunning, multi-award winning Grenache Shiraz Rosé' but all of the wines have done exceptionally well in wine shows. The emphasis on varietal character in the wines has been essential to the success of the wines. The 2008, 2009 and 2010 vintages of the Rosé won a total of 4 trophies, 8 Gold, 5 Silver and 13 Bronze medals. The 2009 vintage was awarded the Trophy Best Rosé at the Sydney International Wine Competition 2010, Top Gold Medal at Brisbane Wine Show 2009 and Top 100/Blue Gold at the Sydney International Wine Competition. The 2010 vintage was awarded Silver medals at the Concours Mondial De Bruxelles 2011 and Decanter World Wine Awards 2011, and a 'Category Champion' Award at the Wine Access International Value Wine Awards Canada 2010. Reviews have focused on the vibrant colour and flavours of fresh berry fruits and spice and a crisp, dry finish, referring to the wines as 'carefully crafted', 'stylish and dramatic' and one reviewer said it was 'simply a knockout'. The Rosé has scored 90–94 points and five stars in reviews.

The first three vintages of Nine Vines Viognier won a total of 2 Gold, 3 Silver and 13 Bronze medals and regularly scored 85–89 points in reviews. The two reds, Shiraz Viognier and Tempranillo Shiraz, have also been well-received. The 2007 and 2008 Shiraz Viognier won a total of seven Gold Medals, and the 2008 Tempranillo Shiraz was awarded 'Best Other Red' at the 2009 Hyatt South Australian Wine Awards. The wines have scored 88–93 points in reviews. The 2010 Pinot Grigio was awarded a Gold Medal at the 2010 Royal Adelaide Wine Show.

Organic

In mid 2008 Angove Family Winemakers released their first organically grown and produced wines, Shiraz/Cabernet and Chardonnay. The company had been promoting minimal chemical intervention in winemaking for some years and this approach has extended to their vineyards and those of their growers. The organic range is produced in accordance with Australian Organic Standards (2009) and is certified by Australian Organic Certifiers Pty Ltd. Under this certification, no synthetic chemicals have been used in the vineyard during grape growing or in the winery during winemaking.

Tim Boydell commented, 'The organic range has been hugely successful and has received very good reviews. In May 2009 *The Big Red Wine Book* gave us the best organic or biodynamic wine in Australia. But even before this, I was with our reps in Sydney; we went to 13 stores and all of them bought the wine – that's very unusual. The wines are very good, they love the packaging and the fact that 'Organic' stands out – you might say it ticked all the boxes. The organic wines are beginning to enter the export market. The EU has special requirements to call a wine organic, as does the USA and Scandinavia, and all are different. But, we have already had interest from the USA through our partners there. I think it will be a great success for the company and will be a great part of our future viticulture.'

Warwick Billings commented, 'There's huge interest in the organic area. The Riverland climate is perfect for organic production as the disease pressure is so low and though it's still to be completely proven, that by being organic the grapes do slightly better in a hot place. Nick Bakkum has enthusiastically embraced the process and it's going well.'

Long Row

The Long Row label was introduced in 2002 and has been a highly successful range of wines. It replaced *Classic Reserve* which had been produced for over 15 years, mainly using fruit from Nanya Vineyard. Classic Reserve did well in the marketplace but there were problems with the trademark. It was not possible to register the words *Classic Reserve* as they were just descriptive and could not be used as branding in Europe where these words have specific protection. The Long Row name drew inspiration from the redevelopment of Nanya Vineyard which was, in effect, making the rows very long – 5 km

The **Long Row** range has been awarded many accolades and medals since their first release. In the three years 2007 to 2009, the Long Row Verdelho has won two trophies, one Gold and 10 Silver and Bronze medals. The 2008 Long Row Merlot won a Silver Medal and 'Best in Class' at the International Wine and Spirit Competition in London, and the 2008 Long Row Riesling won seven medals including a Gold Medal at the 2009 Riverland Wine Show, and the 2010 Riesling won a Silver Medal at the 2010 New Zealand Wine Show.

[3.2 miles]. Warwick Billing recalled, 'In 2002 we made some very good wines; it was a cool vintage, and so the marketing team jumped on that, saying we can do the name change over with these wines. Long Row probably took longer to get established than we expected but now it's doing well – often heralded as the best value quality wine under $10.'

Fruit for the Long Row range is sourced from Nanya Vineyard and long-term contract growers in the Riverland and other regions of South Australia including the Limestone Coast. The wines in the range are Chardonnay, Sauvignon Blanc, Verdelho, Riesling, Shiraz, Cabernet Sauvignon and Merlot.

When reviewing the Long Row wines, wine journalists consistently make statements such as 'over-delivered on quality', 'go beyond expectations' and 'remarkable value'. The company's attitude to making these wines was reflected in comments by Jeremy Oliver in *The Australian Wine Annual 2008*, 'I am particularly impressed with its winemaking attitude, which is to attempt to create the most elegant and balanced wine possible, regardless of the ultimate price of the finished product.'

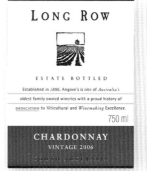

Red Belly Black

The Red Belly Black range was launched in 2002 and takes its name from the Australian Red-bellied Black Snake, which has a deep purple-black body, and a vibrant red-orange belly. The label was developed with the USA market in mind and it has established a good presence in this market. The range of wines comprises Chardonnay and Shiraz, produced from grapes grown in the cool Limestone Coast region (Wrattonbully and Padthaway) and in the Riverland. The wines have won numerous awards at Australian and international wine shows. The most recent releases (six vintages) of the Shiraz have been awarded a total of 3 Gold, 4 Silver and 16 Bronze medals.

Bear Crossing

The Bear Crossing range of wines was introduced in March 2001 and has been a huge success in the export market. Each bottle sold provides a donation to the Australian Koala Foundation, which, in the first two years, benefited by $100,000. The 2002 Bear Crossing Chardonnay was named 'Best Value White Wine under $10' in *Quaff 2003* and the wines have continued to do well in wine shows.

The development of the brand name was not without its problems, as John Angove recalled. 'It was originally going to be Koala Crossing but there were trademark issues with another company regarding the word 'koala'. They've now changed the law and you cannot own names like koala or kangaroo – it is no longer possible to register iconic names. So, we went to Bear Crossing and got heaps of criticism about koalas not being bears. We decided to put a tag on it saying that for every bottle of Bear Crossing sold we would give five cents to the Australian Koala Foundation – they were more than happy.

Butterfly Ridge

Dr William Angove was a noted naturalist with a special interest in ornithology and butterflies. The name of this range recalls a locality just north of Tea Tree Gully where he observed and collected butterflies. The first wines in this range were introduced in 1994. The range which comprises Colombard/Chardonnay, Shiraz/Cabernet, Merlot/Cabernet, Riesling/Gewurztraminer and Chardonnay, are 'bright, lively wines', designed for current drinking.

Evolution of the Butterfly Ridge label 1994 to the present

Sparkling Wines

Angove produces two naturally sparkling wines, Regent Brut (Non Vintage) Chardonnay Pinot Noir and Zibibbo, a luscious, lively wine with floral and spice aromas. Zibibbo takes its name from the southern Italian name for the grape variety Muscat of Alexandria. In 2010 the Stone's family of products was extended with the introduction of Stone's Gold, a low strength (8% alcohol) ginger-flavoured sparkling wine.

Studio Series and Chalk Hill Blue

The fresh, flavour-filled wines in these ranges are specifically selected for the restaurant and café sector of the market. They are intended to complement a broad range of food styles.

Fortified wines

As beverage wines have increased in popularity, fortified wine sales have significantly declined. Angove continues to produce a range of fortified wines which include Angove Premium Vintage Fortified Shiraz and the Bookmark range. The Premium Fortified Shiraz is only produced in exceptional vintages. The 1996, 1999 and 2005 vintages have won significant awards at wine shows.

The company ceased making their **Marko Vermouths** in 2008, bringing to an end 80 years of production. John Angove commented, 'In the 1970s we sold more vermouth than just about anything. Vermouth was our No 1 product due to the substantial increase in spirit excise and the popularity of cocktail drinking at the time. It was seen as an alternative to expensive spirits; sales grew dramatically, but then declined. There were long lead times for buying herbs from overseas and there were problems in making small quantities, especially dry vermouth, which needs to be fresh. Smaller batches were made but they seemed to last longer and longer.' Everone concerned felt unhappy about having to make the decision to cease production but as Warwick Billings observed, 'If the market is not there, there's no point in making a product that people don't want to buy.'

Another long-standing brand that has been discontinued is the **Fino Flor Dry Sherry**. Once a very popular style, sales were declining and with stock not moving the potential to compromise quality was becoming very real. Warwick Billings commented, 'It wasn't moving through the shops fast enough, therefore it was not fresh enough, and that's very important for a product such as Fino. We stopped production and the plan was always to reintroduce it at cellar door, which is perfect as we can guarantee it was bottled in the last six months.

'There's quite an investment in producing Fino. We agreed to keep the technology, the knowledge, as it's a dying art in Australia and when the outlet reappears we will be ready. You can't build a solera that takes five vintages over night. You can start selling as you build it up though. Another good call but yet to come to fruition.'

Stone's Green Ginger

Stone's Green Ginger Wine continues to be a very important part of the company's portfolio. It is very well-known and popular in both Australia and New Zealand and is found in virtually every bottle shop in Australia.

In 2001 Angove launched Stone's Ginger Beer. They had been considering developing a ginger beer for some time but it always seemed to be too difficult. Finally, they approached South Australian Brewing Company to produce a fully brewed beer. As John Angove said, 'It has done very well in the market place, and continues to do so. The introduction of the ginger beer has pushed the parent brand along very nicely. We've discontinued Stone's Exhibition but we still make Stone's Mac. Stone's Reserve was introduced in 2006. It is slightly higher in alcohol and has a very strong, almost burning, ginger punch. The latest addition (2010) to the range is Stone's Gold, a ginger flavoured sparkling wine.'

The Stone's ginger wines have a dedicated following amongst consumers and its production offers a different sort of challenge to winemakers, according to Angove's former winemaker, Warwick Billings.

'From a winemakers point-of-view it's a fascinating product. We only made batches a few times a year. It's broadening as a winemaker because you get to taste lots of gingers and see which are the good ones. We prefer the Australian ones because they taste so good. Some of the others have all sorts of strange flavours, a breadth of flavours that you don't normally associate with ginger. We use a dried, fresh ginger from Buderim Ginger Limited in Queensland.

Paul Ritchie, of Buderim Ginger, commented, 'Angove prefers our late-harvest product, July to August, when the oils and essences are at their peak. We dry it in a special oven and vacuum pack the ginger in bales for delivery to the winery.'

Concerning Stone's Red Label Reserve, Warwick commented, 'We spent quite a bit of time developing that product. It's a good wine, quite hot, and I think it should be in every cook's cupboard!'

Tulloch Wines and agency brands

ESTABLISHED 1895

TULLOCH

In 2002 Angove Family Winemakers took on the distribution of Tulloch wines from the Hunter Valley, New South Wales, and have since acquired a financial interest in the company.

J.Y. Tulloch & Sons was established at Pokolbin by John Younie Tulloch in 1895 and by the 1920s was the largest vigneron in the Hunter Valley. The Tulloch family sold their Glen Elgin vineyards and winery in 1969 to the UK-based paper group Reed Consolidated Publishing and later, following a series of changes in ownership, it became part of Southcorp Wines. In 2001 Southcorp decided they no longer wanted the brand. Ross Pitts, a Sydney businessman and owner of Inglewood Vineyards Pty Ltd at Denman, and Jay Tulloch bought the brand and they then developed the new company as Tulloch Wines.

John Angove continued the story, 'They approached us to distribute the wines in Australia. Tulloch had a strong presence in New South Wales and we needed a stronger product in that State. We saw the distribution as complementing our existing activity, particularly in New South Wales. It was working well and then Ross asked if we wanted to put some equity into the company? Inglewood Vineyards Pty Ltd is the major shareholder and the Angove and Tulloch families have equal shares and other smaller holders have the balance. We distribute the wines Australia-wide and Tulloch Wines handles the export market.

'All of the wines are from the Hunter Valley. Sales of the Verdelho are very strong in the New South Wales market where the brand is well-known but it is growing in Queensland and Victoria. The Tulloch range has done well in wine shows and the Verdelho has been outstanding. The last eight vintages have been awarded 3 Trophies, 5 Gold and 13 Silver or Bronze Medals.'

Agency brands

Angove started to handle agency brands in a small way in the 1980s, notably Suntory from Japan in July 1985. This aspect of the business has grown considerably in the past decade to the extent that agency lines now constitutes approximately 25% of the company's top-line sales.

A former Marketing Manager at Tea Tree Gully, Markus Evele, commenced the development of new agency arrangements for the company. The early agency lines included Glenfarclas Whisky and Perrier-Jouët Champagne.

The expansion of agency lines occurred in part because of Angove's marketing structure. Tim Boydell commented, 'We set up our own distribution network in Australia so we could be masters of our own destiny, but it was costly to operate and for it to only sell Angove wines it was a very expensive way to achieve our goal. Our industry is very much about people and relationships. We decided to build other income streams, find appropriate agency partnerships to provide a service and to add income streams to the company. We also wanted to make ourselves more valuable to our target market, particularly the chains and independent retailers.'

Partnerships have been forged to expand the company's portfolio of wines. The agency brands marketed by the company (as at 2011) are Tulloch (Hunter Valley), Shingleback (McLaren Vale), Mount Riley and Gibbston Valley (both from New Zealand),

Left: Customer Service Officers – (L to R): Caroline Taylor, Nicole Vallelonga, Maxine Leedle

Right: Marketing – Rosemary Porter, Marketing Assistant, and Michelle Slater, Trade Brand Manager

Above: Export Administration – Natalie Horvat and Kim French

Moss Brothers (Margaret River), Turkey Flat and Charles Cimicky (both from Barossa Valley), Temple Bruer (organic wines from Langhorne Creek), Wicks Estate (Adelaide Hills), Water Wheel (Bendigo), Nicolas Feuillatte and Palmes d'Or Champagne (France), Villa Jolanda Prosecco (Italy), Glenfarclas Whisky (Scotland), and Quinta do Pégo Ports (Douro Valley, Portugal).

Most of the companies with which Angove is associated both in Australia and internationally are family-owned and operated.

Glenfarclas whiskey is distilled by J. & G. Grant, Speyside, Scotland; the company is owned by the fifth and sixth generation of the Grant family – John and his son, George. It is one of just a couple of major distilleries in Scotland that has remained independently owned. The company has always bottled its product as single malt. The Glenfarclas 30 Year Old was judged the 'Best Single Malt' at the inaugural Malt Whisky Society of Australia Challenge in 2008 and again in 2009.

> Glenfarclas offers the largest range of single malts imported into Australia, and celebrates its 175th anniversary in 2011.

John and Lyn Buchanan and family own and operate Mount Riley Wines Ltd at Blenheim in the Marlborough district of the South Island of New Zealand. Their vineyards in the Wairau Valley were established progressively from the 1980s and their wines are renown for their superb quality. Angove have marketed their wines since 1996 and a strong relationship has evolved over this time. The other New Zealand label that Angove markets in Australia, Gibbston Valley, is from Central Otago.

Champagne Nicolas Feuillatte was founded at Chouilly, Epernay, France in 1976 and has grown from a small family vineyard to become the largest selling Champagne brand in France and the third largest selling brand in the world. The agency includes the Nicolas Feuillatte and Palmes d'Or ranges of Champagnes.

Paramount to the agency arrangements is to have a good working relationship. Tim Boydell said that the agencies work well because of this: 'I think that's why the Trinchero – Angove relationship in the USA is getting stronger and stronger – we are both family businesses. AMKA Vinimport, Denmark, who distribute for us in Scandinavia – they cover nine countries – was started from scratch by Karsten Sondergaard, so he's first generation, but now he's handing over to his son, Frank. It's a strong family business. We find we have better, longer, stronger relationships with family businesses.'

Richard Angove took over Matt Redin's role in the management of the agency lines after seven years in the role in 2008, and said, 'We have a good diversity of wines. They are important in giving our sales team greater options for offering to retailers and restaurateurs.'

Wine marketing

None of us can do well unless we know what the challenges are. It's not about what you know in business, it's about what you don't know so you can get help in those areas. To know where your deficiencies lie is generally important.

John Angove

The *domestic market* for Angove wines has grown very strongly over the past decade. As John Angove observes, 'The domestic market is around 65% of our business. I'm comfortable with that; I would be much less comfortable if 85% of our market was overseas, due to the present uncertainties that exist with the export trade.'

Angove Family Winemakers has sales and marketing people based in or responsible for all Australian States and Territories. Customer Services was relocated from the interstate branches to a central location at Renmark in July 2009 and the staff at Renmark service wine orders for all of those branches.

Tim Boydell, Director of Sales and Marketing, and David Dalton, National Sales Manager, are based in Sydney and Matt Redin, National Marketing Manager, is in Adelaide. David Dalton coordinates the regional sales managers and export to New Zealand, while Matt Redin is responsible for consistency across the company's marketing and promotion. His role has been helped greatly by the adoption of Angove Family Winemakers appellation. The culture of the business has changed. As Matt related, 'The sales and marketing people meet together along with the winemakers and vineyard people. Discussions across areas of responsibility didn't happen in the past. We all did our own thing and didn't know what anyone else did. There's a whole cultural shift that John [Angove] has brought to the company. It's really a family winery; John is responsible for our families as well as his own, in the broadest sense. Our people refer to our vineyards, our winery, our wines – the staff have a true sense of ownership.'

Matt Redin initially joined Angove Family Winemakers in 1997 as a sales representative. He studied wine marketing at the University of Adelaide and worked for a time at Petaluma Wines as a vineyard and cellar hand. He left Angove after 18 months

Staff at Renmark, Christmas 2010

and worked in wineries in Oregon and California. He returned to Angove in 2001 as Brand Manager, based at the Tea Tree Gully winery. This was just when the company was starting to change direction. 'The sales team was changing and John [Angove] was moving towards being a wine company and developing brands we could sell globally. It is a slow business turning a company around but we've done so.'

The last few years have been rewarding for Matt and the sales people. He says that it is good getting comments from wine journalists such as, *Angove is a hidden sleeper, one to watch*. 'This builds our reputation and confidence and it rubs off onto our sales people and to their customers. We are doing things that are innovative, a bit different and this takes us beyond being just another winemaker.'

Australasian Sales Manager David Dalton holds similar views. When David joined Angove as Sales Manager for New South Wales in 1987, the company was still seen in the trade as an old family company producing brandy, fortified wines and bulk table wines. 'When John Angove interviewed me for the position, he already had the focus to change the company's image. It's now a very different company from within than it was then and the trade is starting to see this.

'Angove is regarded by the industry as a company with integrity. The company has a good name and is trusted; these are pluses in hard times. John takes the company's reputation very seriously and is careful to guard the business' good standing. It has stood the company in good stead when you think that just 10 years ago the corporates were saying companies of our size wouldn't be in the market in a decade's time. They were very wrong.'

When David joined the sales team in Sydney, Ken Stevens was State Manager for New South Wales. Ken retired in September 1994 after 30 years with Angove (he then served as a Board member from 1994 to 2003). David assumed the State Manager role that also included looking after the accounts with the major liquor chains. He was later given responsibility for the New Zealand market. Over the past five years the company has become more nationally oriented whereas previously the State branches were pretty well autonomous operations. Finance and ordering is now centralised at Head Office at Renmark and each Australian State has a Sales Manager who is responsible for their sales representatives.

Ron Howard joined Angove's in September 2002 as Regional Manager for South Australia, Western Australia and Northern Territory with some 25 years' experience in wine marketing. He had worked for a large corporate wine company and had to readjust to working for a family-owned company. He considers that he joined Angove at the right time. 'It was the end of a period of generational handover of the company and significant production changes were underway. The major changes involved reworking Nanya Vineyards and moving into premium wine production.'

*Matt Reddin (National Marketing Manager) and Tim Boydell
(General Manager Sales and Marketing) at Tea Tree Gully*

Export markets

Angove Family Winemakers is currently exporting to 35 countries and, according to figures published by the *Australian and New Zealand Wine Industry Directory*, is number eight in the Top Ten of exporters of labelled wine in Australia.

Tim Boydell is Director of Sales and Marketing. 'Our greatest market concentration is North America, UK and Europe, but there are a number of emerging countries – India and China – that are a longer term goal as their drinking habits are changing from spirits to wine; but it has enormous potential.

Regarding their growth in the export market, John Angove observed, 'We've followed the wave of the industry through that incredible growth overseas driven by the wine industry's goal of a billion dollars of export business by 2000. That goal helped focus the industry and during the 1990s we had a great time shipping wine around the world. Demand was strong and supply was weak, price was almost what we named. The industry went through great growth but the top of the curve was in about 1997–1998 and it has been on a decline since then. Supply caught up and in the UK the power to squeeze prices has increased strongly.

'Margins in the UK trade went from being good to totally disastrous. Now at the bottom end of the market, wine is being supplied from the surplus, but when a balance returns, Australia will have to reposition itself. It will be a demanding process.'

'In the 2009 vintage we, and a lot of other producers, pulled back substantially in tonnage because we knew large accounts were likely to disappear. Overhead factors will have to be spread over less litres of wine but we won't be putting such blatant red ink on the bottom line. Exports will be extremely tough as the global oversupply continues.'

The United States of America has become a well-established market for Angove Family Winemakers. In 2005 a long-term arrangement with Trinchero Family Estates was agreed. Tim Boydell commented, 'In about 2002, we identified a need to re-align our winery with a more powerful U.S. partner and that was when we learnt that Trinchero was also looking for an Australian wine partner. We invested an enormous amount of time and energy to get this arrangement established, ahead of a number of other Australian wine companies.

'What I believe was a critical factor in our success was the unique synergies across all levels of both businesses. Trinchero is a third generation family-owned and operated company and has very similar business values to Angove. We got along well at the personal level and both parties could see that a solid, long-term relationship was achievable.'

Mario Trinchero, his wife Mary and brother John purchased the Sutter Farm Winery in California's Napa Valley in 1948. The family business has succeeded much like the Angove family through hard work, ingenuity and integrity.

The creation of White Zinfandel in the early 1970s and the introduction of high-quality, affordable varietal wines in the following decades have made Sutter Home the second largest, independent family-operated winery in the United States.

Jonathon O'Neill has been one of the Regional Export Managers since 2008. He had worked in wine marketing with wineries in Australia and in the retail trade in England prior to joining Angove. He is responsible for the UK and Europe and sees his main role as getting Angove wines 'further up the value chain to give a better return. There's not much in it for the producer if you're retailing at £4–£5 a bottle.'

Critical to Angove Family Winemakers' success on both overseas and domestic markets is the accreditation to the prestigious British Retail Consortium Standard, encompassing ISO9001:2000 HACCP and Environmental components. Regarded worldwide as a benchmark in the quality standards, this accreditation affirms the company's position as a producer of wine and brandy products of the highest standard. Angove was the first Australian winery to achieve this accreditation to Higher Level Status for the entire operation at Renmark.

Many distributors have been working with Angove Family Winemakers for a long time. 'AMKA in Denmark has been distributing Angove wines since about 1990. The markets vary in what they take. AMKA, for example, take our whole range.

'Most of our customers visit Renmark from time to time and we show them the winery and our vineyards. We also take them to other wine regions where we source fruit.'

As to where recent changes at Angove sit with future export markets, Jonathon is most encouraged, 'The volume game is not where we want to be. We now have wines that we produce less than 1000 dozen; it helps us to offer so much more to our customers. It's about broadening our offer to include small, interesting parcels of complex wines. We've received lots of accolades in recent years and this recognition is rubbing off onto our customers.'

Angove Family Winemakers exports to 17 countries in Asia, Middle East and the Pacific. Prospects for growth in China and Japan look good but will take time to develop. John Angove commented, 'We have a new link in China, Mercuris, established by Victoria Angove. Brand development in China will be a very long-term, slow process. In Japan where we also have a new contact, Toa Shoji Co. Ltd, is showing strong potential. Hong Kong, Malaysia, Singapore, the Philippines are all progressing. The Philippines has been quite strong for us, through Wine Warehouse Corporation run by Brett Tolhurst who came from the South Australian Riverland, so he had some affinity with what we were doing.'

Canada is regarded as a challenging market in which to sell wine. John Angove commented, 'Our distribution there is run by Ivan Klobucar who has been with the company for over 30 years. He is now based in Canada and also handles sales in some European countries. Dealing with the Liquor Commissions is difficult. We do reasonably well in Alberta and British Columbia, dribs and drabs across the Prairies and the east, Nova Scotia and New Brunswick. Ontario and Quebec, the big markets, are difficult. In the United States, the harder you work, the more you get, but in Canada, hard work does not necessarily yield any result if the Liquor Commission decides against your brand.'

Angove has had a presence in the New Zealand market for many decades. Sales are largely dependent on Stone's Green Ginger Wine. Their agent, Nick Hern of Vintage Wines and Spirits in Auckland, handles Stone's and some of the wines. Australasian Sales Manager David Dalton sees New Zealand as a challenging market. 'Obviously, we would like to see our wines become more prominent. The majority of our sales remain the Stone's Green Ginger range, including the Ginger Beer. We sell some fortified wine and table wines, bottled and in bulk to on-premise outlets. It is a tough market, partly because New Zealand import lots of wines from all over the world – good wines from Europe and South America – and their own industry has grown hugely in the past decade. But, importantly, we do have a presence there.'

Changing approaches to management

Many aspects of running the Angove business continue to evolve. The office at Renmark was redesigned during 2005 and was completed in December of that year. The original timber-panelling has been retained and incorporated into a modern office facility. Modern technology has replaced many of the office procedures of the past.

Company Secretary Andrew Coombe joined Angove in 1984 as Senior Accountant. His family were fruit-growers at Renmark and Andrew studied accountancy at the University of Adelaide. Andrew has been a Director of the company since November 1999.

During his years with the company it has grown considerably. 'The company has tripled its annual turnover in my time. Tom Angove saw survival as very important having been through the Depression and a World War. We've now gone beyond that in some ways but it gave us a very strong structure or platform from which to build.

'Angove was a traditional wine company based on fortified wines and brandy and then in the 1960s took on Stone's which ended up having a life of its own. This gave us a broader base than other companies that were purely based in table wines. It has probably made Angove more resilient in tough times. It wasn't all that long ago that people were saying that mid-sized wineries would not last the distance. But, we've made a presence in what we do and we're very professional. We appeal to people who want something real.'

> The wine industry is all about the mystique of wine and industry history – Angove has a real story, real substance.
>
> *Andrew Coombe*

Of his years with the company Andrew said, 'Things change all the time. It's an exciting company to be with. It's a family-oriented company – you feel a part of the company and that you can contribute. I've been more than lucky.' That's a sentiment returned by the management who value Andrew's skills and input very highly.

Company Accountant Trevor Gill joined Angove in January 1974 straight from secondary school and now assists Andrew in his role. Former company secretary Bob Abbott encouraged Trevor to study accountancy which he did part-time for five years, completing the course in 1979. Trevor handled the company pay packets. 'Employees were weekly-paid and it was in cash. It was a lot of work but I personally knew every employee then.

The company's first computer came in June 1979 and that area has advanced in leaps and bounds. We had four accountants in the office, one of whom was Gienus Doevendans. We did the payments to our grapegrowers – around 180 of them – many are very loyal suppliers. I also looked after the affairs of Cole & Woodham until the franchise business was sold.'

The Office Manager, Frances Dunhill, joined Angove in December 1983 as a receptionist and later became Personal Assistant to Tom Angove, John Angove and Andrew Coombe. When she joined the company there were 13 people in the office. Multi-skilling and the computer system have reduced staff numbers, but in addition to those people are the export and IT people. Michael Darby is responsible for the computer system which is used to record a host of things that were previously done manually. Much of the paperwork for the interstate branches was handed to the individual branches but during 2009, this was centralised once again at Renmark. As the Office Manager, Frances also has a role in areas such as OH&S, Workers' Compensation, Quality Assurance documentation and the production of a quarterly in-house newsletter.

Another area of change has been that of Occupational Health and Safety, combined with employee relations and quality control. Jo McConaghy was Angove's first Human

Administration office, March 2010 –
L to R: John C. Angove, Andrew Coombe, Mark Ramm, Natalie Horvat, Frances Dunhill, Stewart Celani, Kim French, Derek Martinson, Kathy Anspach, Trevor Gill, Michael Darby, Jo Stone

Resources (HR) person and undertook a lot of the groundwork to get systems in place and to organise staff training. She also had responsibility for negotiating with the unions and for enterprise bargaining. Claire Angove commented, 'Jo had a lovely warm personality and encouraged people to work with her in what was then a very new area.'

When Jo began at Angove in 1996, employee involvement in most decision-making did not exist. Jo had come from a background where 'input from anybody on any level was welcomed and consultation was the name of the game; it was quite a shock; almost like stepping back in time'. However, Jo recalled, 'John recognized the need to *take everybody* along on the journey of change and the need to change the culture of the organization. The recognition that an HR position was called for was a huge step forward.'

'I recall my first SWOT – Strengths, Weaknesses, Opportunities, Threats – analysis of the HR areas within the organization, listing the length of time that many employees (including senior managers) had been with the company, as a threat, one could have heard a pin drop. A newcomer was anyone who had less than seven years of service. I saw the lack of new blood and thus new ideas, style and perspectives, as a real issue.'

Not daunted by the task ahead, Jo set up consultative groups throughout the organisation to establish how best to engage the employees and move the company forward. 'In the early days the consultations were simply long lists of complaints, but as employees saw issues dealt with, and things changing, we did start to see good input from the floor. Communication training sessions were held with both management and employees participating and I believe these bore fruit. In the early days it gave people a common language with which to communicate.

'Training programs were embraced throughout the organization and all employees, from the vineyard to the sales staff, were given the opportunity to attain trade level and higher qualifications. No longer were dead men's shoes awaited; if employees had the initiative and were prepared to do the necessary work they could earn the status and the financial rewards. This, of course, gave the company a greater knowledge base and more informed workforce to take forward.'

To assist in breaking down the barriers the company took part in local events such as the Renmark Pageant. After a couple of years Jo joined the senior management team, only to find that meetings were totally formal affairs. 'They were not the most fruitful environment to ensure effective communication between department managers. I'm glad to say over the next few years a less formal, more frank and effective environment developed and management meetings became an effective communication tool.

'In saying this, I'm not being critical of the previous style of management, it suited the era but an autocratic style of management was difficult for somebody of my generation to understand. Mr Tom Angove – and his father before him – led the company during times of great difficulty and it survived various economic and industry ups and downs – that's no mean achievement.

'John's management style was great – one just got on with the job and occasionally he gave you pointers on the map to follow. One absorbed his visions for the future and his ethics by osmosis. He allowed a great deal of personal freedom and gave an enormous amount of trust. His stewardship has prepared the company so that it could cope with Gen X and Gen Y'ers who are so important today. The way his children have been brought into the organization thoroughly prepared for the path ahead is great.'

Jo left Angove after 10 years with the company. 'I look back on my years at Angove as a time of great change for the organisation; to change a culture is not easy but it was accomplished thanks to John's vision for the future.'

The HR process that Jo put in place has continued and currently Joanne Stone who joined Angove in 2005, has responsibility for all aspects of the business relating to 'human relations and quality systems'. She observed, 'Quality control is done differently at Angove from other places I've worked. Quality control is divested to everyone in the company. We all have a responsibility. I have an overseeing role; if there's a non-conformance, I track it down and rectify it. We use a positive approach to things – we have a problem with something, so how did the system fail and how can we prevent it from reoccurring?'

'The company sees staff training as very important. Often it is part of grooming someone for a new role in the company or it might be apprentices attending trade's school. Training has been offered in diverse areas, such as food processing, management, technical and computer programing. Our staff has really grown in their abilities – training is very positive. I think this reflects the way employees feel about working for a family company. They have said to me that the prosperity of the company is their prosperity. There's a lot of ownership amongst the staff. They know that what they do in their work has a direct impact on the business.

'John's management style engenders this feeling about being part of the family. I was the second person to come to Angove from another wine company; there is now five or six of us all from the same company. One of them once said to me, "John said hullo to me by name when he was walking through the cellar." I said, "Yes – and …", to which he replied, "You'd never get that at my previous job." John likes to know the staff, what they do and how they are getting along. It's important not just being seen as a number.'

This comment is echoed by Neale Dunhill, Works Manager, who observed, 'In other firms you work for someone you never see, and you have two lives, work and private. At Angove, when you walk through the door you don't forget your family. They enable you to do things during the day to do with family needs. You are part of the business and they look after you as a family member.'

Cellar door sales –

Top left: Caroline Taylor and Linda Thiele

Bottom left: Leonie Tyck, Natalie Horvat, Michael Darby

Centre: Roger Wyatt (R) in former cellar door sales area at Tea Tree Gully

Cellar door

The cellar door sales areas at Renmark and Tea Tree Gully have both been relocated and redesigned in recent years. The sales area at Renmark was moved into one of the original wine storage buildings. It has an old winery look about it but is modern in its décor. Alcoves have been used to divide up the company's range of wines and their agency lines which, makes choosing wines easier for cellar door visitors. The impressive timber counter was built on-site by the company's carpenters out of jarrah timber from old, decommissioned storage vessels.

The cellar door outlet at Tea Tree Gully was moved to the former function room in the original winery in 2004. Roger Wyatt managed the operation of cellar door sales, assisted by Jane Hawkins. The new sales area was larger than the previous site and was well appointed. With the sale of the Tea Tree Gully property, the cellar door was closed on 15 October 2010. Roger Wyatt retired at the same time after 41 years of valuable service to the company.

South Australian Adelaide office team 2011 –
Back (L to R): Michelle Slater, Jonathan O'Neill, Victoria Chaplin, Ron Howard, Sandy Soppit, Richard Angove, Lean Kosir,
Matthew Redin. Seated (L to R): Rosemary Porter, Belle Godden

AFW Victoria office team 2011 –
(L to R): Carmen Dienhoff, Craig Healy, Pat Gilbert, James Blackwood, John Solyom, Sheryl Gannan, Courtney Goodman,
Antony Bristow and Adrian Marsili. Absent: Paula Read

AFW Queensland team 2011 –
Back (L to R): Vanessa Claudatos, Cassandra Skinner, Yvonne Murray, Adrian Paine, Lorraine Graham, Jeffrey Davison.
Front (L to R): Janie Kocev, Lea Rickwood, Sean Trotter

AFW New South Wales team 2011 –
(L to R): Brad Charters, Paul Langbein, Cameron Colville, Stel Cusmiani, Jeff Dibble, Donna Bourke, Michael Riitano, Adam Hollway, Wayne Marshall

Celebrating 125 years and beyond

'John's desire is to pass the business on to the next generation, the legacy and the history. He feels a strong responsibility to the immediate community at Renmark, and to the industry that he has backed so much over the years.' Tim Boydell

As Angove Family Winemakers marks its 125th anniversary as a family-owned and operated wine business, they are proud of their past but are strongly focused on the future of the company. Over the past two decades, John Angove, as the fourth generation of the family to manage the business, has implemented a huge investment in winery and vineyard infrastructure to maintain the continual improvement in the quality of their wines and spirits, and to ensure that the business is in good health for successive generations. Angove has an experienced Board of Directors that guides the company and continues to promote its position as a progressive winemaker and producer of premium quality wines.

The Board

The current Board (2011) comprises John Angove (Chairman), Victoria Angove, Tim Boydell, Andrew Coombe, Gienus Doevendans and Bruce McDougall, an external director. Bruce McDougall worked with Southcorp Wines as an agricultural-horticultural manager and is now a wine industry consultant with various companies. John invited Bruce to join the Board. 'Bruce has been a great contributor, and is very interested in what we are doing. He has been very much a part of our moving forward.'

Bruce commented, 'I've brought an external view to the company which is what John was looking for. Angove has a solid capital base which is often the case with family-owned companies, is conservatively run, and has great resilience. It is not servicing shareholders and can take a long-term view of things. It is useful to have a non-executive director to put points of view, especially to family members on the Board, which the other directors may not do.'

He sees the major achievements during his time on the Board as the fostering of a generation succession strategy and the coming together of the grape-growing and winemaking aspects of the business. 'Continual improvement is the thing. The momentum has really picked up in the past five years. I think management has given people the ability to show what they can do and has stimulated them to do it.

'It is important to keep investing in the business, in our people. There is a real focus on personal development – technical, skills training, occupational health and safety, a new area of emphasis. Similarly, in marketing, we engage with our major customers on a personal level.'

'I feel that the Board functions well. We can sit around the table and divorce ourselves from our executive roles, especially Andrew and Gienus, for instance. Tim Boydell has become a very important cog in the system. He came to us in 1999 as an export manager working out of Tea Tree Gully. He very quickly showed his ability to do more than be an export manager and this happened to coincide with our National Marketing Manager being taken unwell; so, we put Tim into that role. Then he came on to the Board, in November 2002. He has been very instrumental in driving us domestically. He is a very strong contributor and we owe him a great deal.'

Gienus Doevendans was a Director from November 1999 until his retirement. As one of the company's longest-serving employees, he spent about the same amount of time with John as Managing Director as he did with Tom. Gienus commented, 'They have handled the company very differently, but you'd expect that. Tom never shirked responsibility. He was there to make sure things happened and, at the end of the day, he took the responsibility. The company was much smaller then than it is now and you just couldn't run it that way today. John takes the approach that responsibilities need to be shared down the line. Department managers used to report to the owner, but now they report to Operations managers who meet each week with the Managing Director.'

The McLaren Vale Vineyard

As part of producing premium fine wines, Angove Family Winemakers purchased a vineyard at McLaren Vale in 2008. Sourcing fruit from various regions of South Australia lead to discussions about the possibility of buying vineyards in other regions. As John Angove related, 'I was always interested in the Adelaide Hills, especially the Eden Valley area, and then with the progressive demise of the Tea Tree Gully area – the loss of the vineyards in the 1970s and the scrub behind the winery site and more recently the winery site itself, there was really no

reason to be there, other than history. So, when we quit the Tea Tree Gully site altogether, the logical thing would be to establish another near city site we can call home.'

The company looked at properties in the Adelaide Hills and McLaren Vale and eventually considered the latter was the better option. An established 10 hectare vineyard was purchased from Tinlin Wines of McLaren Flat. The vineyard was mostly planted to Shiraz, with smaller areas Cabernet Sauvignon, Grenache and Merlot. It is managed using biodynamic principles.

A cellar door sales and function facility is being developed on the property and is due for completion by the end of 2011. 'The McLaren Vale vineyard will grow in its contribution to The Medhyk, our premium red wine, and it will assist in continuing to generate our profile as premium winemakers.' The design for the cellar door and function centre incorporates a replica of the original Brightlands Cellar, as a link with the company's origins.

The vineyard and winemaking team are excited about the prospects of the new vineyard. Winemaker Tony Ingle said, 'The vineyard has a variety of soil types and microclimates, and I'm working with Nick Bakkum and Richard Angove to investigate and develop the differences in those characteristics that we see in the finished wines. The first wines have been bottled ready for release and we are very pleased with them; we think next year's releases will be even better.'

After a number of years of planning and discussions, Angove sold their St Agnes Winery property at Tea Tree Gully on 30 October 2009. John Angove said that the decision to sell the property was a difficult one. 'It is the last connection to Dr Angove and his establishment of the company on the site in 1886. But, with the demise of the vine-

yards in the 1980s and the removal of all winemaking and storage over subsequent years, the economic worth of the site was hard to justify simply for offices and warehousing. I see the purchase of the McLaren Vale vineyard as a replacement for the Tea Tree Gully vineyards and sales outlet and *The Medhyk* brand – *medhyk* is Cornish for doctor – as a continuation of a link with our Cornish founder, Dr William T. Angove.'

Tea Tree Gully Council's heritage requirements mean that some aspects of the winery will remain, in particular the original winery building and the distillery tower. The tower has long been a well-known local landmark.

Following the property sale, the Adelaide office was relocated in October 2010 to the former Romalo (originally La Pérouse) sparkling wine cellars on The Parade, Magill.

Industry contribution
and recognition

John Angove has continued the family's tradition of involvement in wine industry bodies. John said, 'I virtually took Dad's spot on the Wine and Brandy Producers' Association and then I kept on getting re-elected! I have enjoyed the involvement – it has kept me engaged with other industry people.'

John has been a member of the Association's – now known as the Winemakers' Federation of Australia – Management Committee since 1988 and the Executive since 1992. He has been chair of the Wine Industry Technical Advisory Committee 1993 to 2011 and Chair of the Brandy Sub-committee 1993 to 2007, at which time its activities were included in the Technical Advisory Committee. He was the President of the South Australian Wine Industry Association from 2006 to 2009, and a Board member of the Australian Wine Research Institute from 2010.

The company's association with teaching and research into wine and spirits saw it provide support for the Angove Still House at the Hickinbotham Roseworthy Wine Science Laboratory at the Waite Campus of the University of Adelaide in 2003. The still house featured glass pot and continuous stills for research and teaching, and an Italian-manufactured small production-scale copper pot still, with 400 litres capacity. John, Claire, Victoria, Richard and Sophie Angove attended the opening of the Angove Still House by Sam Tolley, the then Chief Executive, Australian Wine and Brandy Corporation, on 2 May 2003.

In November 2005 John Angove was named the Riverland Winemaker of the Year. He was awarded the title at the Riverland Wine Show in recognition of his outstanding contribution to the Riverland's wine industry, including promoting the region's wines overseas and raising exports of his own family business' brands to become one of the largest exporters of Australia wine. In the New Year's Honours 2011, John was made a Member (AM) in the General Division of the Order of Australia in recognition of his contribution to the wine industry and a range of arts, conservation and charitable organisations.

Over the past decade, Angove Family Winemakers has received enormous recognition for the quality of its fine wines and brandy. It is significant that show awards and critical acclaim has been across the range of Angove wines, not just for the premium labels. The integration of grape production and winemaking, and the care and attention taken during winemaking has seen the company reach a new level of excellence.

Angove Family Winemakers was named 'Winery of the Year' in 2007 by *Quaff 2008 – Best Wines in Australia under $15*. Peter Forrestal of *Quaff* said of the award, 'Angove is the deserved winner of our Winery of the Year Award, although they faced tough competition from Yalumba and last year's winner, De Bortoli. The improvements at Angove were evident last year but the quality of the wines has continued to get better and their performance over the past twelve months has been exemplary.' The Long Row Chardonnay and Cabernet Sauvignon were named 'Best White/Red Wine under $10'.

In May 2009 Angove Family Winemakers' wines were acclaimed in wine-writers Campbell Mattinson and Gary Walsh's *Big Red Wine Book 2009/10* and the company was named 'Recession Busting Winery of the Year'. To quote the authors, 'Given the economic climate this year's *Big Red Wine Book* took a more "budget" view of wine, and launched a special award for the winery best equipped to help wine consumers through it. Angove is that winery. If ever there were a time for a special award, it's now, and if ever a winery deserved it, it's Angove Family Winemakers. Wine after wine, whenever we tasted Angove red it made us do a double-take. Some of the wines are under $10, most are under $15 and pretty much all of them are under $20 – and they're all good. This is recession-busting red winemaking at its brilliant best.'

The authors stated, 'Early in the research for this book it became clear that Angove was in the running for the Red Winery of the Year award. Its consistency across the board is stunning.' Twelve Angove red wines scored between 86 and 91 points (out of a possible 100). The *Big Red Wine Book* was particularly impressed by the Organic Shiraz Cabernet 2007 (91 points): 'This had us floored. There's a very strong argument that organically (or biodynamically) grown vineyards tend to produce high-quality wine … This thoroughly delicious wine proves that organic excellence can be achieved affordably – which isn't just good news for consumers, but is good news for the industry, too. Buy some!' They went on to say, 'This is certified organic and it's very good. We have a feeling it marks a new era for high-quality, affordable organically grown red wine in Australia.'

In conveying this news to the company's employees, Matt Redin concluded his message with, 'Huge praise to all involved at all levels in the vineyard and winery. The paradigm shift continues.'

Gienus Doevendans was appointed a Director of the company in 1999, a post he held until his retirement at the end of June 2011 after 46 years of service.

Gienus' career was the classic story of the school leaver who joined a company and made good through ambition, hard work and dedication, eventually rising to be a Director, a rare thing in today's ever-changing world.

Into the future

With 125 years of winemaking experience behind the company, Angove will continue to value and develop their broad portfolio of fine wines and brandy. The company remains proudly independent and family-owned and operated. The continuing success of the company is in no small way due to the ongoing support of all who work or have worked with the company over its long history – employees, grape and industry suppliers, agencies and retailers – and consumers both in Australia and around the world.

John Angove's view of the future for the industry in general is covered by his comments: 'I think the future challenge for the Australian industry is to maintain our position as a quality wine producer. We have got to maintain that edge both in quality and perception of quality over the other new world wine producers in particular, and over the Europeans in due course as well. I think, on average, Australia produces the best wines in the world. I think you can go out there and find superior wines, but you cannot find the depth or the extent of the quality through the volume that Australia produces. It's second to none, and we've got to retain that.

The Angove family in 2010 – (L to R): Richard Angove, Victoria Angove holding daughter Emily Amber (first of the 6th generation), John Angove, Claire Angove, Sophie Angove

John, Victoria and Richard Angove, March 2011

'The greatest challenge for Angove is to continue to develop our presence as a significant player in the winemaking world. We've come a long, long way in a fairly short time and we've got to build on that, so that when people think of Australian wine, they think of Angove along with the other quality winemakers in the industry.'

In its 125th year, Angove Family Winemakers is producing premium quality wines from some outstanding vineyards. Its wines and brandies continue to win significant awards. The company has an enormous source of expertise in its employees, people who have a strong sense of ownership of the company and their role in it. The Angove family is very proud of their family heritage as winemakers and the company's image as a traditional but progressive and innovative maker of fine wines and brandy.

The company's long-standing values and its commitment to producing quality product will continue to bring it success and accolades. Future directions are difficult to predict, but then nothing much has changed in that regard since the company's founder, Dr William T. Angove, planted his vineyard and produced his first wines 125 years ago. There is little doubt that Angove Family Winemakers will continue to play a significant role in the evolution of the Australian and global wine industry.

Looking to the future – John Angove with grandson Henry

Acknowledgements

I am most appreciative of all the people associated with Angove Family Winemakers who have helped me in the compiling of this 125-year history and I commend the Angove family for wanting to record the story of their wine business. The early history of the family and company was largely compiled when writing *Mining, Medicine and Winemaking,* published to mark the centenary of Angove in 1986. Valuable assistance was given by many of those listed below and other people including Dr Roger Angove, Mrs Dorothy Angove, Mrs Mary Barker, Mr David A. Thomas, Messrs Bob Abbott, Cyril Brady, Dennis Hall, Robert Hill, Gil Hamister, Bill Marshall, Max Steinwedel, Colin Haselgrove, Bill Hockey, also Mrs Cora Hall, Mrs Kate Nightingale and Miss Mary Whillas.

In the course of writing the present book, the following persons were either inter-viewed and/or provided information: family members – John C. Angove, Claire Angove, Thomas W.C. Angove, Beverley Angove, Victoria M. Angove, Richard R.C. Angove and Sarah Angove; company employees, present and past – Nick Bakkam, Warwick Billings, Tim Boydell, Shane Clohesy, Andrew Coombe, Leanne Cosir, David Dalton, Andrew Darby, Gienus Doevendans, Frances Dunhill, Neale Dunhill, Trevor Gill, Jim Godden, Ray Goodes, Ron Howard, Tony Ingle, James Kelly, Jo McConaghy, Bruce McDougall, John Norman, Jonathon O'Neill, Rosemary Porter, Matt Redin, Joanne Stone, Roger Wyatt and Nick Yap.

Photograph credits

(t = top; b = bottom; r = right; l = left; c = centre)

Angove Family Winemakers' Collection – ii, iii, x, 2, 3, 4, 5l, 6, 10, 11,12, 13, 15, 17, 18, 19, 20, 21, 22, 24, 25, 26, 28, 30, 31, 32, 34, 35, 36, 37, 41, 45, 47, 49, 50, 52, 55t, 121, 132, 133, 134: all wine labels

Photographs by Dr W.T. Angove – 4t, 5r, 6, 13

Geoffrey Bishop – 7, 9, 40, 53, 54, 55b, 64 tr tl bl bc, 65tr bl lc, 66, 68, 69, 73, 77, 78l c, 79r l tc, 82bl cb, 83cr cb tr tl, 85, 87, 88, 89, 124, 128, 131, 137, 139

Aspect Photographics (Kevin O'Daly, Clay Glen, Mark Zed) – 55br, 64tc c, 65tl tc c bc br, 71, 77br, 78r, 82tr tl c cr br, 83tr bl, 90, 93, 100, 121, 131c, 136r

Italo Vardaro/ Vardaro Studio – 65lc, 79bc, 92

Simon Casson – vi, 72, 74, 76, 80, 83c, 95, 103, 122, 140l

Brett Hartwig – 97, 140r, 141

Advertiser Newspapers Ltd – 61, 105

The University of Adelaide – 98

Index

....

Wakefield Press is an independent publishing company
based in Adelaide, South Australia.
We love good stories and publish beautiful books.
To see our full range of titles, please visit our website at
www.wakefieldpress.com.au.